MAN AS HERO

THE CLASSICAL AMERICA SERIES IN ART AND ARCHITECTURE
Henry Hope Reed and H. Stafford Bryant, Jr., General Editors

W. W. NORTON & COMPANY, INC.

The American Vignola by William R. Ware

The Architecture of Humanism by Geoffrey Scott

The Classic Point of View by Kenyon Cox

The Decoration of Houses by Edith Wharton and Ogden Codman, Jr.

The Golden City by Henry Hope Reed

Fragments from Greek and Roman Architecture The Classical America Edition
  of Hector d'Espouy's Plates

The New York Public Library: Its Architecture and Decoration by
  Henry Hope Reed

Monumental Classic Architecture in Great Britain and Ireland
by Albert F. Richardson

The Library of Congress: Its Architecture and Decoration by Herbert Small

What Is Painting and Other Essays by Kenyon Cox (in preparation)

WITH THE ARCHITECTURAL BOOK PUBLISHING COMPANY
Student's Edition of the *Monograph of the Work of McKim, Mead & White, 1879–
1915; Letarouilly on Renaissance Rome:* The Student's Edition of *Paul Letarouil-
ly's Edifices de Rome Moderne* and *Le Vatican et la Basilique de Saint-Pierre* by
John Barrington Bayley; *Architectural Rendering in Wash* by H. Van Buren
Magonigle (in preparation)

*Drawing of the Classical: A Videotape Series devoted to the drafting of the Five
Orders* by Alvin Holm, A.I.A. (in preparation)

Classical America is the society which encourages the classical tradition in the
arts of the United States, Inquiries about the society should be sent to Classical
America, in care of W. W. Norton & Company, Inc., 500 Fifth Avenue, New
York, N.Y. 10110

MAN AS HERO

The Human Figure in Western Art

PIERCE RICE

W · W · NORTON & COMPANY

New York   London

Copyright © 1987 by Pierce Rice
All rights reserved.
Published simultaneously in Canada by
Penguin Books Canada Ltd.,
2801 John Street,
Markham, Ontario, L3R 1B4.
Printed in the United States of America.

The text of this book is composed in Bembo, with
display type set in Bembo. Composition by Vail-Ballou Press, Inc.
Manufacturing by The Murray Printing Company
Book design by Jacques Chazaud

First Edition

W. W. Norton & Company, Inc.,
500 Fifth Avenue, New York, N.Y. 10110
W. W. Norton & Company Ltd.,
37 Great Russell Street, London WC1B 3NU

1 2 3 4 5 6 7 8 9 0

For Marilyn Young Rice

The Publication of *Man as Hero* was made possible by a gift of Mrs. John Cleaver of Milwaukee in memory of her husband and a grant from the Oliver Grace Foundation.

Mr. Rice wishes to acknowledge that *Man as Hero* owes its existence to Henry Hope Reed, the president of Classical America, whose encouragement kept him, over a long period of time, at the typewriter.

   Mr. Rice would like to give special thanks to the following people who helped considerably with the details that have gone into the making of this book: Diane O'Connor for expert assistance with matters of production and format; Ruth Mandel for her picture research campaign, H. Stafford Bryant for editorial supervision, and Julia Ballerini for editorial assistance.

Contents

List of Illustrations

———

LIST OF ILLUSTRATIONS

MAN AS HERO

The Human Figure
in Western Art

Some of us find it gratifying, others are simply forced to admit, that at this late date the world takes guidance from American example in matters of art.

In this area we have always been less than challengingly defensive. We admire our famous artists but are uncertain about just how famous they actually are. Is there a Parisian alive who would recognize the name of Winslow Homer? *Whistler's Mother* is in the Louvre, and that museum is supposed to own, as well, a picture by Thomas Eakins. Two pictures perhaps, one for sure. One need not bother to look for the American section. But the issue is one on which we do not feel very strongly. What we would like is a little respect. Apart from that, we share the European view and do not see, much less claim, any real comparison. We are, after all, Europeans ourselves.

What it comes down to is that we are an equivalent of the Greeks in Sicily, finding ourselves, in effect, located abroad by the merest circumstance of history and geography. As Europeans we are not even competitive, never mind defensive, in relation to other cultures. It simply does not occur to us to make comparisons. This is half vanity and half an instinctive sense that the distinctions involved are not measurable. In the 1920s Oswald Spengler, in his *Decline of the West,* caused a stir, and not so brief a one at that, with his contention that the gulfs between cultures, distant or vanished, are uncrossable. The novelty of this theory has long expired, but perhaps, for all that, it is true.

We are all charmed by sphynxes, scarabs, lotus leaves, but except that they come from the banks of the Nile, which of us knows the least thing about them? Specialists apart (whom we take on faith), we cannot tell one falcon head from another, though they were created a thousand years apart. If we could, with an effort, detect differences, there would be no clue for us as to which of a pair was the older. The idea of development in Egyptian art, of primitiveness, of fulfillment, of decadence, simply defeats us.

As much holds true of art further east. Chinese painting, anonymous to begin with, sculpture, pottery, architecture, calligraphy, strike us as all of a piece, from far before the Christian era to the present. The wood-block prints from Japan that so captivated the Western world in the nineteenth century had been turned out in quantity for the popular market. When Japanese painting made its appearance, it did not effect the regard in which the wood-block prints were held. A distinction glaringly apparent to the Japanese themselves failed to register on the European (or American) eye.

Before we trouble ourselves over the problem so posed, another consideration asserts itself. In the absence of extraneous information, of dates, of artists' names, of questions of originality versus duplication, might not our enjoyment be all the purer? When the lecturer straightens us out a little in the matter of schools or techniques, is our pleasure not actually diminished, or at least diverted?

And in being struck most forcibly by the sameness of the artifacts of an exotic style, are we not brought closer to the culture's central core than the recognition of subtleties would allow?

Without making an effort toward that end, we really do possess general ideas about Islamic art, African, Central American, Assyrian, Scandinavian, that earnest investigation (or what the scholars could tell us) would only refine. What is to be remarked on is that we have a much cloudier perception of the fundamental nature of our own art. Nor is there any reason to think that the factors described here fail to hold true at home. That is, that in being all too conscious of the extraordinary variety of domestic creative activity, and the circumstances attending its production, both present and past, our enjoyment is more impeded than not.

It is not being said here that we prefer the strange to the familiar; that would be contrary to human nature. But it is all too true that the art on which we must, after all, depend for our spiritual nourishment exerts its effect on us only over obstacles. And the first of these obstacles is that our attention is arrested by the differences between individual works rather than those great factors in common which give unity to a culture, that, in the examples we have been discussing, account for a homogeneity seemingly lacking in our own.

The impulse might be to say that the art of the West is peculiar to itself in that it is without common factors, but that would go against the law of the world. We cannot claim to be that independent of history and the nature of things. Art is not really freer than language, or physiognomy, or the animal kingdom, from connection with its place of origin. Whatever difficulties there may be in identifying it, there is no possibility of the West being without a style.

If we glance again at the art of ancient Egypt, we are struck, of course, by its peculiarities of treatment, but we identified it to begin with by a very limited range of themes. And, in fact, the two, technique and subject matter, are inseparable. Egyptian art is unimaginable except in terms of both. That is, unless the familiar processional arrangement, the two dimensional drawing, and the stylized movement are employed in conjunction with rams' heads, the serpents, the solar disks, and the rest of the slender cast of Egyptian characters, the method itself is unrecognizable as Egyptian.

The contention here is that this is as true of ourselves, that there is a great central Western theme, placed before us in an envelope of form as binding as that of any other culture. Entirely apart from the actual evidence in the matter, no other hypothesis is tenable.

To make some order out of even a tiny random sample of Western works of art is of course impossible. To find a pattern in the works by which most store is set, the masterpieces, would not tax a child. At the risk of ours appearing the vainest of all societies, it has to be acknowledged that its principal preoccupation, as expressed by the efforts of the greatest of its creative minds, has been with ourselves. The supreme subject has been the celebration of Man. Every triumph of brush or chisel extolls humanity.

Insofar as the argument needs to be demonstrated, it becomes stronger as we become more selective; the loftier the masterpieces examined, the more apparent the case. The pictures and statues that have most moved us through the ages have depicted a race superior to ourselves in stature and grace, but akin to us.

INTRODUCTION

That it was not until very late in history that there was such a thing as secular art, that originally a carving was itself the god portrayed, is no more than the anthropological explanation of the matter. What we are concerned with is the visibly godlike attributes of pagan and Christian art alike. A quasi-religious character remained affixed to art in that the images shown us were what might be called inspiring by example. Physically, from their being prepared for particular places, they possessed a good measure of the nature of the altar. The portable picture or statue was a late development.

The ostensible subjects were the heroes of mythology, kings and queens, saints, prelates, gods, God, soldiers, angels, the once and still famous, but collectively of enduring interest as an aristocracy of vast distinction of bearing. The identification of the actual individuals and the episodes they take part in is secondary to their universal character.

For the heart of the matter is idealization and generalization. We focus now on the idiosyncracies of those we admire, but it was not always so. Through most of history, artistic treatment meant improvement of the model. The portrait itself was a resemblance only among other things. Not least, carriage and movement were of far greater consequence than characterization. There was, too, a mechanical consideration. Sculpture was primarily architectural, so there was a premium on large, as opposed to particular, forms. In turn, painting was of a pronounced sculptural cast. But the physical requirements enhanced, rather than hindered, pictorial purpose. Breadth lends itself to beauty.

The archteype of the idealized, generalized, natural form is the Greek female profile. Instantly recognizable, she is

La République on French coinage, Liberty on ours (long ago, that is), the young Queen Victoria on British. Hers is the head most frequently to be found on European statues and, never mind Neo-Classicism, she fills up the canvases of the Renaissance, the centuries of the Baroque and the Rococo, and had a good run well beyond those times. But this beautiful device no more than illustrates, in the universal use made of it, the nature of artistic practice at large.

For the Western designer depended as fully as any other on an existing body of conventions. This was supplemented by that study of life itself that gives Western work its vitality; but what moves us not only in the great examples but in the body of work in general is the combination of stylization and observation. If there is a secret underlying the magnificence of European art it is the maintenance of the balance between the two. The decline, when it came, was due to, or demonstrated by, the weakening of that balance.

It is the strength actuality provides that gives plausibility to an exalted view of the world. By the same token it is the use of symbols refined by time in the recording of what the artist sees that gives his vision its esthetic character.

So much for the instruments of the glorification of the human figure. That glorification itself is the great hallmark of the style. Other pictorial elements contribute to this—the likely architectural setting, the condition of light, the glimpse, or more generous view, of landscape, the subject's garments and accoutrements—but these remain subordinate. The fold in a garment, or a distant cluster of farm houses, from the brush of Correggio, could by themselves almost bring us to tears, but the intense charm of his main actors prevents us almost physically from turning our attention even in passing to these ravishing details. Rembrandt's mysterious illumination has by all means aroused curiosity and admiration, but never at the expense of the object of that illumination. In the great orchestrated works the order of things imposes itself.

In a peculiar sense, painters and sculptors improved to their own detriment. The public became so captivated by the sumptuous decoration of the Renaissance that the few who could afford it wanted, in effect, samples for their private delectation. This led first to the diminutive, or movable, version of projects originally intended for permanent installation.

Harmless, or even beneficial, as this might appear it was a blow to the hitherto exclusively public and civic character of art. The picture or statue that could easily change hands, and that was customarily displayed as an end in itself added nothing to the beauty of the community, and by the diversion of talent it represented, detracted from that beauty.

There was an even more adverse development. What had been the minor parts of heroic works presently became the principal subjects themselves. The still life, the landscape, the architectural study, in their independence, first acknowledged the primacy of the figure, and then reduced it to their own level. There was a step beyond this. The paint, the pencil mark, the surface of the stone, became of more consequence than what they described the appearance of.

What has been recounted here is often construed as progress. And it is true that when it first occurred to an artist to paint and frame a little bucolic scene complete in itself the door was opened to a wonderful source of plea- 7 sure in the centuries to follow. And as much can be said of still life. But while a few great spirits could impart nobility to mundane subjects through the power of design and style, this was not the main path taken. When every subject was assigned equal value, none had any, and the very roles of painting and sculpture in our lives came into question. Not least, in a democratic age, they became the exclusive concern of the elite.

It should be added that in the trivialization of theme, and the cutting off of painting from the ornamental task, the ancient bonds between painting and sculpture and architecture were severed, which had been the chief source of strength for each of them.

In the alien cultures of which we comprehend so little but are so fond of, there is a lesson for us. When they succumb to outside forces, they maintain their wholeness. They do not, of their own accord, jettison the harmony that is at the heart of their appeal. Egypt was overwhelmed by Hellenism. The other ancient cultures expired with their societies. Those of today, for all their political independence, are falling prey to our artistic ideas. What is lamentable about the new cities that spring up in the desert is not that the buildings put up by the American engineers are so bleak, but that, with the wealth available, gorgeous Moorish fantasies were not brought to realization. But this is quite other than a deterioration of the Islamic forms themselves. Eastern art may or may not still be practiced, but it has not, like ours, become difficult to define.

In that sense, in the unambiguous distinctness of their styles, these far away, or long vanished, civilizations are superior to our own. To put ourselves on the same plane (much less assert a supremacy with which we instinctively

8

credit ourselves) we will have to emphasize not the great individualities that we harp on at home, but the shared characteristics of our supreme achievements, which we have singled out as the celebration of Man, or in literal terms, the human figure. But for the championing of this concept to be other than a nostalgic exercise (which would assume the Occidental culture itself to be simply one more of those lost in the mists of time) it must be advanced as the dominant, live, critical test of artistic performance.

Prevailing doctrine, of course, runs directly counter to the thesis roughed out here. Duncan Phillips, the collector, some years ago gave forth with the pronouncement that: "There are no leaders and followers; there are only artists and pretenders." This dismisses in an insufferably patronizing phrase the attaching of any seriousness to the practice of art at large. But however repellent in tone, the statement represents what might be called the operating viewpoint of the twentieth century. The premium is on the distance a given artist can establish between himself and his predecessors and contemporaries, with this the test of individual attainment.

Every artist of power distinguishes himself from his fellows, but if that distinction is the principal goal of his (and all artists') efforts, the larger aim of general harmony, the indispensable ingredient of beauty on any scale, is put out of reach.

The formidable body of argument that supports the theory of the assertion of personality as the artist's chief duty could be disputed point by point, perhaps, or perhaps not, convincingly. But that would be to examine the subject through the wrong end of the telescope. Our concern is with entire societies and peoples, seen, so to speak, horizontally, across the breadth of whatever portion of the earth they occupy, and latitudinally, as far through time as they maintain a visible cohesion. So viewed, the individual artist is of consequence only in the contribution he makes toward the overall unity that identifies not himself but a major section of humanity. The measure of his worth is the degree that he strengthens and increases that unity.

In regarding art from a perch so distant that entire schools and nations are ranged side by side, an immediate question advances itself: Is not the fundamental issue one of religion? In the vast body of the accumulated creative effort of the world, only a tiny portion is purely secular. If we appear, in recent times, to be doing all we can to redress that balance, the matter of the survival of secular art is still very much up in the air; thus, the weight of it fails to alter our assumption. Art is far older than history, but the idea of it, independent of a spiritual application, came very late.

It might be added, as to the secular character of contemporary artist and society alike, that the abandonment of its immemorial role as principal patron of the arts by the church is by all means a factor. What we know nothing of, after all, is the spiritual inclination of the artist himself through history. All we are certain of is that religious art is what was almost exclusively required of him. In that light the matter would have nothing to do with painters and sculptors, everything to do with society.

But if it would appear to follow that a believing people is most conducive to a flourishing art, and that toward this end religion should be encouraged, an absurdity is introduced. We can wish for an artistic revival, or a religious one, but not reasonably for the latter if our actual goal is the former.

10   At the same time there is every reason to suspect that

any number of religious works were commissioned, even by the clergy itself, out of an interest in the artistic rather than the spiritual side of the result.

In this connection, it might be noted that pagan subjects in statues from pagan times are, except technically, no different from the same subjects depicted in statues of the Renaissance. And those pagan themes are treated by the later artists not a whit differently from Christian ones.

Rubens is the ideal case in point. Religious himself, the fact of that played no part in the division of his professional attention. This division is difficult to measure from the scale of his output, but lists of plates in the countless books on Rubens would seem a fair indication, and there the breakdown is close to fifty-fifty. This is after deducting those pictures—portraits, hunting scenes, landscapes, odds and ends—which are neither pagan nor Christian. When these are included, outright religious subjects amount to about a third. The main point is that everything is treated alike. The *Death of Sennacherib* can be distinguished from the *Death of Decius Mus* only by close examination. And what this suggests is that, to patron and painter alike, the nominal subject was not the actual one. What concerned Rubens, and fascinated his public, was the human body in dynamic movement, with the specific dramatic activity this movement contributed to remaining entirely secondary.

A similar case could be based on Titian or Poussin. And what is to be made of the Sistine Chapel, whose (admittedly few) detractors found the work of its devout decorator wholly pagan?

Historians make much of the fact that Chardin and Watteau were admitted into the French Academy by, so to speak, the back door. As a pair, they might perfectly well be advanced as the supreme painters of the eighteenth century. Yet their colleagues, whose names would only faintly survive their own times, could see fit to allow these two to sit alongside them only under special conditions. That is, with the proper field of the painter taken to be history, room could be made for humbler practitioners, but with a qualification. What are we to think of the likes of Largillière graciously pontificating along these lines?

In fact, there is not the least sign that Chardin and Watteau failed to subscribe to the principle invoked. That is, each had elected to work on a lower level than that which all parties, themselves included, acknowledged to be the noblest. Nor is there anything in this the least unusual. In our own era, how many choose statesmanship over salesmanship, or write poetry rather than advertising copy? In the eighteenth century itself, never mind still life or fêtes galantes, the gifted carvers of France turned out infinitely more mantlepieces and vases than statues.

What is of consequence is that the distinctions of theme were clear to everyone, with the question of merit entirely independent of this.

To go back a generation, however beautiful a landscape by Claude Lorrain might be conceded to be, it would have crossed no one's mind, even Claude's, that it was to be compared with a sacred or pagan canvas by Poussin, or, to emphasize the point, Simon Vouet or Eustache LeSueur.

Backward as all this may seem to us, it is to be noted that this was the outlook of an age incomparably superior to ours in creative matters. If we are more generous in our judgments, it is also true that liberality is the sole superiority we can claim, and that is not an artistic factor to begin with. It is but one more example of the substitution of moral for aesthetic values.

12

The odd circumstance is that we do, habitually, establish classifications. As much as we lionize the stars of the stadium or stage, and complain over the quality of our political leaders, we do not really equate Babe Ruth with Lincoln or Washington. And, perhaps unfairly, all work is categorized in ways too obvious to mention. Not least, the artist as such is put on a pedestal wholly without reference to his talents or accomplishments, and fine art itself on a plane above applied art.

In that light, the view we are encouraging is more natural to us than not. In fact, the jumbling together of every class of work of art, with excellence the supposed test of order, is perfectly foreign to the normal working of the mind. What we recommend here goes against nothing but prevailing convention.

If we could, accordingly, bring ourselves to recognize the divisions that we have suggested the existence of, not the least rejection of anything we are fond of would be entailed, but the atmosphere would be marvelously cleared. We would remain free, as their contemporaries were, to prefer Velazquez to Rubens, but it would be apparent that the latter, by virtue of the subjects he dealt with, operated on a loftier sphere.

The examples, then, of painting and sculpture that follow were not assembled to prove the argument as an arbitrary selection out of the masterpieces of the West but, identified for what they are, were simply chosen to illustrate the points made. In pictorial matters, after all, description weighs very little.

Logic might suggest that a choice of works of art confined to the celebration of Man conveys a false impression of the art of the West at large. That is perfectly true, but what is provided here is not an historical record, but a demonstration of the fundamental character of that art, and the contention is that attention to other concerns than the main one only blur that character.

Nor do the landscape, the figure study, the still life, the anecdote, the architectural view, serve as a sort of relief from an overly serious subject. Insofar as there is such an office to be exercised, that is managed within the borders of the true works of art themselves where elements other than the figure simply enhance it by their presence. But seriousness has nothing to do with the question. Man is too broad a theme to be regarded as ponderous. Treatment can be lyrical, dramatic, theatrical, romantic, comic, whatever the mood of an age, or the artist, dictates. That is, we are not dealing with what is deep, or solemn, but what is instinctive and natural.

The argument is not that any number of romantic, or academic, or realistic, or impressionistic, works are not more moving, or beautiful, or skillful, than countless routine accomplishments that more strictly conform to the central current of European art. What is of weight is that the latter, by the mere fact of their existence, add to the wholeness of the visible side of the fabric of Western civilization, while the great works that stir us on narrower premises exert their effect each on its own terms, contributing to no sum total, and in fact detracting, by their strength, from the unity that is the very substance of our (or any) culture.

CHAPTER 1

Definitions

Of all exotic pictorial styles, it is easiest to describe the Egyptian. Moreover, it possesses closer parallels with our own than the styles of societies further east, a circumstance that lends a greater usefulness to comparison. The unvarying processional arrangement, the two dimensional character of individual figures and objects, the ritualized movement, are universally recognizable. Mechanical devices only, what makes them Egyptian is their combination with a fixed set of performers in the Egyptian drama. This cast may not be as limited as it appears, but resemblances register on us more strongly than differences. The rams' heads, the sphynxes, the serpent-crowned profiles, the seated cats, the vultures, establish the style for us with perfect vividness. There are two factors here, form and content, but it is impossible to think of one independent of the other.

What has been arrived at is deducible from any selection of Egyptian artifacts that comes before our eyes. To the pattern laid down, no exception is imaginable. If a slightly unfamiliar character turns up, the seated hippopotamus, say, it is perfectly in keeping with those known to us.

Nothing of this appears to be the case when we give our attention to our own pictorial practice. The range of matter dealt with is infinite. Custom, or even logic, sets no limit on variety of treatment. Anything in the way of a general idea of an occidental view of nature is impossible to frame. Or it might even seem, in a degree of domination by natural appearance that no other system of practice has allowed itself to submit to, that ours is the style most lacking in any trace of style.

We are not quite reduced to that; the picture picked out at random no more represents the art of the West than the utilitarian structures of China have anything to do with the art of architecture, Chinese or any other. The critical view is appropriate; it is only those combinations of forms that succeed in moving us emotionally that qualify as art to begin with. So we are not loading the dice if we turn to the great examples that over the course of centuries have exerted the most power. Whatever else, these works are unquestionably representative of none but ourselves. This is not to say that only masterpieces qualify as works of art—such a statement would be absurd—but that there is no uncertainty involved. Also, once the identifying factors are established, they can serve for the whole body of artistic activity of which they are the culmination.

We may think of the most celebrated works as being unlike as their makers or carvers. Those differences are valid enough, but their resemblances are what count. Granted that, regarded collectively, what we are offered by these pictures and statues is a view of life, the task is to single out what sets that view apart from views of life chosen unselectively, even, and more important, from life itself.

Color is not the area where we should look because color is absent from drawing or sculpture. Nor is design right for our study, because style asserts itself independent from arrangement. A hand roughed in by Gainsborough or Velazquez is as characteristic of either of those masters as the finished picture of which it is a part. A fragment of floral molding from a temple long vanished is as Greek as the temple in its entirety. Beyond that, design exerts its force entirely independent of style. Symmetry, rhythm, balance, harmony, are simply facts of nature, as inexorable in their power over us as gravity, and all artists, everywhere, make equal use of them.

The element we are in search of is, in essence, the reduced masterpieces, deprived of hue and illumination, the physical touch of chalk or chisel or brush, and the distribution of what is actually depicted. The pertinent fact is that, in this austere condition, arrived at by the viewer's imaginative effort, the rough indication in pencil of their forms, or through feeble black and white reproduction, and despite the giving up of a great portion of their charm, the masterpieces remain, as a class, perfectly identifiable. What is left of them, so to speak, are their outlines, and it is those outlines that are the elements we are in search of.

What is immediately to be noticed is that these outlines correspond only approximately with those of the natural forms they are intended to depict. The quirks and accidents that animate actual appearance are nowhere to be found. We are offered, instead, a kind of synthesized view of nature. The continuity of the arm is emphasized, not its interruption by elbow and wrist. The knuckles and joints of the hand are subdued toward the same end. With the human head it is its rotundity that registers on us before individuality. But the limbs and heads themselves are subordinated to the unity of the body itself.

The body, in short, has been so conceived as to bring

it as close as possible to being a single form without sacrificing its human character. The result is a degree of grandeur of aspect far beyond anything we are provided by mere unassisted sight. This graphic loftiness, conveyed by means of the generalized contour, is the hallmark of the art of the West.

Breadth of execution, then, is the indispensable ingredient, but the ennoblement of the human figure, of which this breadth of execution is the instrument, would be so much grandiloquence in the absence of appropriately heroic nominal themes. That is, Man as the subject must be assigned a role infinitely above that of simple studio property. And, in fact, there is, in our own midst, a kind of rough equivalent of the galaxy of mysterious actors that peopled the art of ancient Egypt, and without which that art is unimaginable. This is the loose but not entirely unsystematic roster of characters, real and unreal, or a mixture of both, who have filled out our vision of the world beyond our immediate horizons. These are the gods and goddesses, the elect of the earth, its kings and queens, the philosophers and martyrs, the rebels and champions, the heroes and villains, the creatures of the air, made part and parcel of the furniture of our minds as much by pictures as by history or legend.

This list is unlike that of the Egyptians in that at first glance it appears limitless. In fact, there is little or no range. A single theme here, under slightly varying guises, prevails. A pair of caryatids supporting the lintel of the entrance to a Viennese palace, St. Sebastian lashed to his pillar, Daphne eluding Apollo, wildly unlike in narrative terms, in the plastic arts represent in each case the exaltation of the human body, no more and no less.

A rough parallel has been suggested here with two of the identifying elements of the art of the Egyptians. The silhouette-like character of Egyptian arrangement and drawing is balanced by breadth of contour and a corresponding unity of form, and the hierarchical scheme of gods and pharaohs and attendants by a cast of our own. The element that remains is the unvarying stately pace of the Egyptian protagonists. What we have comparable to that is the grace and grandeur of Western movement.

Our pictures and statues are of a race akin to us, but superior, and carriage and gesture are no less a factor in the suggestion of this than actual appearance. The task of the artist is to indicate nobility and force, while steering clear of histrionics.

The supreme exemplar of what has been put forward here as the fundamental nature of our art is Michelangelo. He is ideal to our purpose because over a long lifetime he found these specifications sufficient to the creation of the most overwhelming individual body of accomplishment in the history of civilization. That is, his immense energies were directed wholly to painting and carving the impersonalized human figure, represented as the chief participants in the ancestral books of Europe, the testaments and the Greek myths, with the majesty and power of his gallery of heroes conveyed by the most stirring physical attitudes ever devised. It should be noted that Michelangelo limited himself not merely to his single august theme, but to the figure unenhanced by setting or accoutrements. He included (and then only rarely) only the most elementary hint of landscape. His Ark, in *The Flood,* and Charon's Barque, in the *Last Judgment,* are as unconvincing boats as were ever painted. Except for their wonderful drapery, his giant creatures are shown to us without any visible possessions. His outlook was so broad that in a career that lasted close to a century he never so much as made an offhand sketch of a likeness.   19

Michelangelo, *The Flood* (detail), The Sistine Chapel, Rome.
Photo Alinari–Scala.

Michelangelo, *The Last Judgment* (detail), The Sistine Chapel, Rome. Photo Editorial Photo Color Archives.

Michelangelo illustrates, rather than proves, the case.

The remarkable fact is that to look at the masters at large reveals no exceptions: More foiled their figures against gorgeous backgrounds than not, infinite care was taken with subordinate detail, concern over resemblance was often evident, but these considerations were secondary. Largeness of vision remains the great common denominator.

It is the hope, in the pages to follow, to make evident the narrowness of outlook along the lines described that prevails beneath the surface variety of the principal artistic achievements of our society.

It should be borne in mind that selection from the work of famous artists adds dramatic emphasis to the thought developed here, but the concern is with identification, not excellence.

CHAPTER 2

The Cherub

That the central theme of the West is Man, with the instrument of this the depiction of the human body at its most splendid, engaged in undertakings of deep consequence, is less oppressive than it might appear. It is gratifying to be able to note that the formula is modified by the presence throughout the art of the past twenty-five hundred years of an army of infants busy at perfectly frivolous tasks. These infants are like their adult counterparts in that they resemble only to a degree actual infants. In particular, the baby of art is a flying baby.

It is proper to designate the child in this way, because his physical character transcends his varying spiritual affinity. Christian or pagan seraphs, putti, amoretti, cupids, are indistinguishable from one another. They are the purest of artistic devices, in the absence of any narrative role, and as much a symbol of the West as the acanthus leaf. More, in the absence of any such phenomenon in actuality, the depiction of the winged infant requires of the artist creative rather than transcriptive abilities. Unlike their human counterparts, barely able to support themselves on the railings of their playpens, the babies of Western deco-

24

ration are in full command of their activity, yet not in the least earthbound. The model is in art itself, and the conditions dictated epitomize the essential nature of pictorial invention.

Examples are everywhere, the merest off-hand product of ornamental practice down the centuries. Nevertheless there are great prototypes. Titian's *Garden of Love* was entirely given over to cupids, and cherubs constitute the whole scheme of the dome in the Camera of San Paolo in Parma by Correggio. Correggio might, in fact, if there is any primacy in the matter, be the principal painter of baby angels in the world, at least in quantity, and almost certainly in the beauty of his version. The somewhat older cherubs supporting the evangelists and saints in the pendentives of the Baptistery and Cathedral of Parma must be the most attractive children ever painted. By contrast, Michelangelo's babies, carrying God on His great errands on the ceiling of the Sistine Chapel, look very grave for their years. But it would hardly do to go into the question of the age of angels. In the various famous depictions of the Assumption and Immaculate Conception the cherubs accompany rather than carry the Virgin into heaven, but the pictures themselves are unimaginable without their presence. If any criticism of these marvelous performances is at all in order, it might be noted that the wonderfully drawn and painted little angels by such luminaries as Rubens and Tiepolo are a good deal less enchanting than those of Correggio, and infinitely less serious than those of Michelangelo.

By the eighteenth century playfulness had become the rule, with Boucher leading all other artists in the volume of cupids produced, and in the effortlessness of their execution. Houdon alone appears to have carved no children

Peter Paul Rubens, *The Assumption of the Virgin,* National
Gallery of Art, Washington. Widener Collection.

Anthony Van Dyck, *The Assumption of the Virgin,*
National Gallery of Art, Washington.

but his own, but it would be safe to say no other sculptor in Europe of the least consequence failed to produce cupids and angels as the very heart of his trade. We are most conscious of them in the Baroque and Rococo churches of northern and southern Europe where in their abundance they are like the stars in the sky. As the century drew to a close Neo-classicism made things difficult for amoretti and putti, but one great master remained unhindered in his employment of the messengers of love. The last great triumph in the genre was from the chalk and brush of Prud'hon whose babies, the match in charm of any ever drawn or painted, were not an offshoot but were central to the body of his work.

Even with the advent of realism, Cupid did not entirely disappear. He was too fixed a hallmark of Western culture for an abrupt demise. Throughout the nineteenth century, if Cupid was rarely to be found in pictures, he continued to play an immense roll in carved and molded decoration. The Industrial Revolution, in fact, may have accounted for more wooden, iron, and china babies than all the Baroque and Rococo artists combined. The immense proliferation of buildings across Europe and the Western hemisphere, and of the contents of those buildings, furniture most of all, with ornament still part and parcel of the structural process, would have seen to this. The difference, and it is not really a crucial one, is that the actual work was from the hands of what might patronizingly be thought of as journeyman sculptors. But the very fact of this testifies to how widespread was the phenomenon.

The last serious attention shown Cupid was on our own shores. It would be fruitless to speculate on the reasons for the enormous commercial and popular success early in the twentieth century of Rose O'Neill's *Kewpies*. It may

Philip Martiny, *America* and *Africa,* detail of the stairway in the
entrance hall, Library of Congress, Washington. Photo Anne
Day.

Philip Martiny, *Cherubs Representing Trades and Professions,*
detail from the stairway in the entrance hall, Library of
Congress, Washington. Photo Anne Day.

have been no more than fondness for babies, but that, as likely as not, was at the heart of the matter to begin with. In any case, working the ancient vein, Rose O'Neill struck a wonderfully responsive chord in the hearts of the American people and enjoyed thirty years of public acclaim, entirely owed to her version of the Antique symbol. An ill trained and commonplace composer, she practiced a drawing never quite free from elementary mistakes, but there was so much life and grace in her every touch and such breadth to her style that, in fundamental considerations, she towered above her contemporaries. However patronizingly fellow artists viewed the Kewpies, the best of her colleagues possessed nothing like the strength her babies represented, far too silly as the antics of those babies often were. It is only fair to note that Rose O'Neill's peculiar power was, in fact, recognized both here and abroad, but this was in connection with drawings of entirely other subjects. When these drawings of the Greek myths were shown, they astonished the critics, but were too far removed from the direction taken in the 1920s to establish their cre-

Rose O'Neill, *Kewpies* from *The Century Magazine,* author's collection.

J. C. Leyendecker, *The New Year*, cover design from *The Saturday Evening Post*. © 1930 The Curtis Publishing Company.

ator as a serious artist. She had to settle for fame and wealth, but it is the country's loss that Rose O'Neill never had the opportunity to make use of her gifts in a form less fugitive than the magazine page.

Another American made it his business to exploit the vocabulary of ornament in a career limited to posters and magazine covers. Trained conventionally in Paris, Joseph Christian Leyendecker developed on his own a complete mastery of the decorative devices of Western art. He had at his fingertips cornucopiae, swags, garlands, cartouches, masks, all of which he painted with an ease and authority beyond that of the foremost of his contemporaries among mural painters. But the most challenging item of this artistic furniture was the winged infant, and Leyendecker made this peculiarly his own. An almost unrivalled virtuoso with the model before him, he retained the same fluency in the improvisation made necessary by the impossibility of keeping a baby still.

It might be noted in passing that it says something about the tone of the times, fifty or sixty years ago, that cupids should, in fact, have been regularly featured on the cover of *The Saturday Evening Post*. Their principal task was to represent the New Year, an office they served from the turn of the century until World War II. It would be a hollow claim on the painter's behalf to relate his accomplishment to contemporary practice. No one else, after all, was painting cupids to begin with. The truth is, Leyendecker's achievement along this line is only to be matched against that of the decorators of the eighteenth century.

CHAPTER 3

The Body
Etherealized

Our emphasis is on the continuity of our culture with the Greeks and Romans, the major part of a single body. It has to be acknowledged, however, that the ancient world has some of the characteristics of an alien society. It was long ago; we know the names of only a handful of artists, and those by legend. Of the surviving works, the question of original and copy is entirely beyond us. We are not even sure the ancients conceived of things in these terms.

These considerations operate not to isolate the treasury of form on which the West depends, but to purify our appreciation of it. As with the pagoda or the minaret our pleasure in the colonnade or the torso is confined to the object itself. The separation from the circumstances that brought it into being makes the pre-Christian, European work of art almost contemporary in its effect on us.

Another factor brings the Greeks and Romans close. From the stylistic identity with ourselves we regard them critically. We feel strong preferences, a faculty that functions very weakly in the case of the genuinely exotic. Not only do we make comparisons between works more or less similar, we weigh the remote past against the last five hundred years, each in their entirety. In this last an objective standard may set the more distant era higher. Our actual affection goes out to that nearer us. The reason, almost certainly, is less our proximity to it than the greater humanity of the later age. The grand impersonality of the Greeks overwhelms more than it moves us. The drama, the warmth, the complexity, one might even say the enthusiasm, of the art of the Renaissance and the succeeding centuries grips us with a force peculiar to itself.

Still, the similarities outweigh all differences between remote and recent past. Where kinship is closest across the span of the thousand year interruption of the Dark Ages is in the theme most free of association with the concerns of life: the most tranquil of all subjects, the unadorned human body, the nude. Moreover, the nude that burst on the world in the sixteenth century was unlike religious art in that it was related only mechanically to the art that preceded it. In conception, the painted nude stemmed directly from the carved one dug out of the Italian soil. The nude, by virtue of this, constitutes the strongest link between the roots of our culture and the modern age.

If we hardly know what to make of the prototype, the Attic nude itself, perhaps that is all for the best. We can examine it in the spirit of those who recovered it. What is surprising is that it was discarded to begin with. Were the Goths and Vandals immune to its charms? Perhaps the very spirit of the nude runs counter to the Christian precepts. The answer is in the province of history and theology. What is left to us is contemplation untroubled by reflection.

The archaic Greek nude has its own beauties, but it was the Hellenistic nude, imported and imitated by the Romans, that determined the course of Western painting

34

and sculpture, and almost by itself accounted for the Renaissance. Its lifelikeness revealed possibilities of execution that stunned the first beholders of these unearthed wonders. Of even greater consequence, it testified to the idea of art containing a spiritual life within itself. Even more than to the matchless surface, that lifelikeness was owed the wonderful animation achieved by the Greek sculptors, a measure of grace that had eluded (or not even been sought by) not only their Egyptian predecessors but every other school of sculpture in the world.

To employ the term "arrested motion" is a feeble way to describe a phenomenon that is outside description. For identification alone, perhaps we should speak of artistic, as opposed to actual, movement. We are limited, really, to illustration. This is fair enough; we are generously supplied. There is no great European figure shown us in a static pose. If this applies to every subject, from devotional works to portraits, it is emphatically so in the case of the nude. The famous *Venuses,* Greek or Italian, win us above all by languorous gesture.

Giorgione's *Venus* is the supreme early example of this, with perhaps next after it his companion Titian's *Venus of Urbino* from a generation later. Beyond these, the temptation is strong to set apart from all the pictures and statues of the world, for sheer beauty of bearing and motion, Correggio's *Io.* But artistic movement is hardly limited to the languorous. The huge figures, clothed or unclothed, that make up Michelangelo's decoration of the Sistine Chapel are properly described as turbulent.

To a degree the gift subsided during the seventeenth century, with grandiloquence given too free a rein. Rubens's nudes, from the quantity of them a class in themselves, epitomize the stridency of their time. This lapse was more   35

Giorgione, *Sleeping Venus*, Staatliche Kunstsammlungen, Dresden.

Titian, *Venus and the Lute Player,* The Metropolitan Museum of Art, Munsey Fund.

Correggio, *Antiope and Jupiter,*
The Louvre, Paris. Photo Musées
Nationaux.

Correggio,
The Education of Love,
The National Gallery,
London.

Correggio, *Danae,*
Villa Borghese,
Rome. Photo
Alinari-Scala.

Veronese, *Mars and
Venus United by
Love* The Metro-
politan Museum of
Art, Kennedy
Fund, 1910.

than made up in the eighteenth century. It fits our purpose that, although Watteau painted one or two little nudes as such, his typical effort along that line was the set of statues he invented as the principal features of the parks that are the settings of his pictures. These beautiful wood nymphs attended by cupids are perfect instances of the etherealization of the human form that is advanced here as the central Western pictorial theme. Watteau nurtured himself on Rubens alongside whom in most respects he remains very slight, but in the area of grace of movement he is infinitely the superior of his great exemplar. Later in the century Boucher would invent an army of statues for his own parks, or what might better be called decorated woods. Boucher was one of the great composers, and these statues serve their artistic office flawlessly, though they fail to approach Watteau's in delicacy.

Boucher's great pupil, Fragonard, would surpass all other masters in combining bold, supremely exuberant action with beauty. The sovereign instances of his painted sculpture are in the Du Barry panels in the Frick Collection in New York City. His contribution to the history of the nude, however, was not confined to garden sculpture. For all their small scale, some of the most magnificent of all outright nudes are from his brush. His boudoir scenes are possessed of so much grandeur of contour, of figures and bedclothes alike, with both exploding in a veritable storm of movement, that they have some claim to recognition as the most heroic of all treatments of the subject.

Fragonard's grand achievement in the vein, his masterpiece in the old-fashioned sense of the word, was the Louvre's *Bathers,* but it was not simply the crown of a lifetime's accomplishment. If we address ourselves to the rhythmic grace of his tumbling figures, we think it must be granted that there is nothing its equal in the whole his-

Tintoretto, *Mars and Minerva,* Ducal Palace, Venice. Photo Alinari-Scala.

Peter Paul Rubens, *Venus and Adonis,* The Metropolitan Museum of Art, Gift of Harry Payne Bingham, 1937.

tory of painting. Challenge can be offered only by the most luminous masters of aesthetic motion. Tintoretto, in his *Origin of the Milky Way,* might seem to have reached the very pinnacle of attainment in this area where skill of any degree at all is rare. Or perhaps Correggio, with Io, but there is an elusive subtlety to the impetuous liveliness of Fragonard's girls that goes beyond even these Titanic examples. There is nothing like this wonderful picture in the way of the distribution of volume. Each individual is

Jean-Honoré Fragonard, *The Stolen Shift,*
The Louvre, Paris. Photo Musées Nationaux.

massively conceived, without the slightest suggestion of corpulence, while it is at the same time part of a perfectly unified form made up of the bathers as a group. What we are compelled to fall back on, to reduce, so to speak, Fragonard to his place, is to indict this marvel for its frolicsomeness. That granted, and acknowledgment made as well of the lack of any touch of poetic pathos or drama, Fragonard's conception is put forward here as the most powerful composition in the world.

Jean-Honoré Fragonard, *The Bathers,*
The Louvre, Paris. Photo Musées Nationaux.

Clodion is commonly represented as the closest in spirit to Fragonard among sculptors. He is a sufficiently great master in his own right not to need the comparison which, in any case, is only true to a degree. Clodion was, for one thing, closer to actuality than Fragonard, but he also had a largeness of vision alongside a measure of boisterous effervescence never reached before or after in sculpture that at least suggests a parallel.

Clodion, *Maid and Cherub*.

Clodion, *Nymph, Satyr and Child Satyr*.

Often classified with Clodion but miles removed from him in taste and intent, Falconet is the very model of restraint and calm in movement. The tiny scale he limited himself to accounts for his being esteemed as a minor master. In fact, the vividness of his modeling, combined with the delicacy of his outlook and the purity of his style, make Falconet one of the commanding figures not only of eighteenth century, but of all sculpture. Falconet and Clodion are but the most conspicuous among an army of colleagues, with the nude very much a staple of the age. The doyen of them all, Houdon himself, produced, almost on the side, three triumphant nudes, *Diana, Winter,* and a *Bather* of his own.

Étienne-Maurice Falconet,
The Bather,
The Metropolitan
Museum of Art,
Bequest of
Benjamin Altman, 1913.

Pierre-Paul Prud'hon, *The Abduction of Psyche,* The Louvre, Paris. Photo Lauros-Giraudon.

CHAPTER 4

The Celebration
of Victory

The ability to depict the figure in action, which might appear to be a natural part of every painter's equipment, has been developed by few, and in those cases by the painter's own efforts. Nevertheless, there was an early and obvious call for the exercise of this peculiar gift. The rendering of violent human movement was essential to the pictorial celebration of military victory. The static figure would not do for war. The challenge was met, and, as of every other subject, beautiful pictures were painted of battles.

If the rigor of physical conflict exhibited one side of the artist's powers, the confusion of it posed the artistic test. The problem was the bringing of order to turmoil. Dramatic to begin with, what we might call old-fashioned war is inherently fascinating to the beholder. By the same token it is the very height of disorder and commotion, hardly to be grasped by the mind and eye. What the artist has to do is offer the viewer velocity modified by clarity. Armed struggle, that is, must be formalized, without being turned into a tableau.

The solvers of the difficulty were among the greatest artists. Taste recommended to Michelangelo that he show the *Battle of Cascina* by depicting his warriors alerted before the onset of their attackers, a solution that to a degree begged the question. In the same hall intended for Michelangelo's never-to-be-completed work, Leonardo da Vinci established the very mold of the European battle picture. In his *Battle of Anghiari,* which we know only through copies, the mounted protagonists swirl and hack away at one another on center stage. That scheme would serve as the vision of war for the ensuing three hundred years. If it appears unduly conventionalized to us, it should be remembered that the principal patrons of this class of picture were themselves participants in the endless series of wars that consumed those three hundred years. What we blithely think of as the Age of Vermeer and Velazquez was really that of Wallenstein and Gustavus Adolphus. Not Watteau, but the most eminent of his admirers and patrons, Frederick the Great, was the paramount figure of the Age of Enlightenment. On the grounds of plausibility we hear of no complaints about this school of art even from that most caustic of critics, Napoleon, whose very home was the battlefield and who commissioned pictures composed to the formula described on a scale beyond that of any other monarch.

We have to acknowledge that in those days a little authenticity went a long way. The soldier at most expected pictures to remind him of his experiences, not show them explicitly. War was seen as the triumph of heroes, even of opposing ones, as in Leonardo's group, where the victor is yet to emerge.

Raphael got the tradition under way with his *Meeting of Attila and Leo the Great,* in the *Stanza of Heliodorus* in the Vatican. Not exactly a scene of fighting, in representing a peaceful success on the Pope's part, it qualifies with its heroes, victorious and submissive, as a record of war. In the *Stanza of the Fire in the Borgo* the *Battle of Ostia* completely fills the bill, without being a picture one cares much for. The archetype of the genre, the common ancestor of all European battle painting, is the *Battle of the Milvian Bridge,* in the *Sala di Costantino.* For the record, the *Milvian Bridge* was the work of assistants, completed after Raphael's death.

Tintoretto's battle frescoes in the Ducal Palace in Venice are, in a kind of rhythmic liveliness, superior to their Roman predecessors, with two of them, the *Capture of Zara* and the *Victory on the Lake of Garda,* fittingly enough for Venice, naval scenes. The first, in its depiction of entire armies, is simply too complicated to grasp, but *Garda* and the *Defence of Brescia* are perfect examples of the type, marvelous glimpses of tumultuous action, with the hero of each a miracle of movement and grace, while very much a part of the action. The authorities tell us that these wonderful arrangements are from the pencil only of Tintoretto. Insofar as that is the case, it testifies all the more to the power of his drawing and design.

Rubens turned out his own version of the *Milvian Bridge,* any number of hunting scenes that stemmed directly from Leonardo's *Battle of Anghiari* of which he had made the best known copy, one or two remarkably unconvincing pictures of the wars of his own times, some martyrdoms and miracles that, in the general uproar accompanying them, could pass for battles, and the great sets of Biblical and Roman stories that culminate in furious combat. All are overwhelming, there being no such thing as an ill-designed painting from the hand of Rubens, but the *Death of Decius Mus,* the *Death of Sennacherib,* and the *Battle of the Amazons* probably illustrate most vividly the type described.

Peter Paul Rubens, *Drawing after Leonardo's Battle of Anghiari,*
The Louvre, Paris. Photo Lauros–Giraudon

Peter Paul Rubens, *The Death of Decius-Mus,* Courtesy, the Princely Collections of Liechtenstein.

This level of thunderous human movement perfectly orchestrated was never to be reached again. A century later, Tiepolo, so consummate a master of action himself, and more at home with the boisterous than any other subject, might have been expected to include a little warfare in his repertoire, but he rarely touched on the theme, and in those cases impressively only by virtue of the general skill in conception and execution displayed. Fragonard, who steered clear of anything sombre or deep, had nothing at all to do with the wars of his time or any other, but among the wonderful little compositions he roughed out in pencil and wash for *Orlando Furioso* were enough sieges and charges and colliding armies to demonstrate the slight trouble anything along that line would have been at a larger scale.

For the record there was an immense increase in the quantity of martial episodes painted throughout this bellicose era, but the pictures themselves suffered from a kind of mindless dependence on the old formula. Revitalization came with the French Revolution, and the liveliest war scenes of the Napoleonic Era were by Théodore Géricault. While still in his teens, or barely out of them, he exhibited at the Salon a series of studies of individual soldiers that, in their spiritedness, outshone the great set pieces of the Imperial victories, splendid as those enormous canvases were.

A generation later, in the equally huge pictures commissioned by Louis Philippe for the Hall of Battles at Versailles, the tradition would come to its end, climaxed by one of the high points of the tradition, the great trio of *Friedland, Jena,* and *Wagram,* by Horace Vernet. Of the three, the finest is *Jena,* dramatic, with just a touch of the anecdotal, and free of any hint of theatrical emphasis. These qualities all three shared. What gives *Jena* its peculiar dis-

Thédore Géricault, *The Wounded Curassier,* The Louvre,
Paris. Photo Musées Nationaux.

Felix Philippoteaux, *Battle of Rivoli* (detail), Musée de Versailles. Photo Lauros-Giraudon.

Denis-Auguste Raffet, *The Reveille,* The Metropolitan Museum of Art, New York. Rogers Fund, 1922.

Denis-Auguste Raffet, *The Nocturnal Review,* Print Division, The New York Public Library, Astor Lenox and Tilden Foundations.

Emanuel Leutze, *Washington Crossing the Delaware,* The Metropolitan Museum of Art, Gift of John S. Kennedy, 1897.

tinction is the inventiveness displayed by Vernet in the figure of Napoleon, seen from the rear, but turning toward the viewer. If Vernet dominates the immensely long corridor of the Hall of Battles not only with these, but Bourbon successes as well, he is at least matched by one other great work, Felix Philippoteaux's *Rivoli*. In this episode from the Campaign of Italy the youthful General Bonaparte of the Directory is presented in terms of as much grace and nobility as the middle-aged Emperor of *Jena*.

The literal last gasp was in the streets of Paris where the lithographs of Auguste Raffet circulated. This great man, a pupil of Baron Gros, with a fluency and power shared by no other contemporary, designed and drew for the popular press a lifelong series of magnificent compositions depicting the military history of France from the Revolution to his own time. Very much within the age-old convention, Raffet's pictures, produced with a stub of crayon on a stone, gave much more of a whiff of actuality than those of his famous predecessors. Beyond that, they were possessed of a degree of poetic invention and wit that makes them, to modern eyes, almost the most satisfactory of all military pictures.

What we have touched on here are the high points of a great line. It is only proper to note that there was an American contribution to this line. Benjamin West's *Death of Wolfe,* familiar to us from childhood, and the *Battle of the Hogue,* a version of which is in the National Gallery in Washington, are both splendid battle paintings. John Singleton Copley's *Sortie of the Garrison at Gibraltar* fulfills in every respect the requirements of the genre. It must be acknowledged, though, that this pair, whatever their origin and their protests, were, or for practical purposes became, Englishmen.

THE CELEBRATION OF VICTORY

The genuine article was John Trumbull, not only very much an American but, briefly, a colonel on Washington's staff. His *Battle of Bunker Hill* might very well be the best known of all American paintings. If it is not, the palm would have to be awarded Emanuel Leutze's *Washington Crossing the Delaware*. The question of superiority is as close as that of their renown. Each is magnificent. Taken together the two paintings are unrivaled achievements in an extraordinarily difficult vein and occupy, accordingly, a very exalted place in the nation's art.

CHAPTER 5

The Personification of Wisdom

We equate the human body, in its pristine condition, with youth. Improvement ceases early. Accordingly, an art that celebrates Man tends to skimp for attention those who are getting on. At the same time the very term, venerable, suggests a degree of deference shown the aged. Perhaps this is owed a superstitious regard for experience or the vague awareness of the stage which awaits us all. In any case, the babies and young people who are the chief staple of painting and sculpture are not exactly balanced, but are at least set off, by a generous selection of graybeards.

The bearded figures in Greek sculpture seem simply to have been intended as adult, not elderly, but in them the mold was set of the Terrible Old Man of the West. The old man as a supreme artistic type, little related to actuality, is Michelangelo's. Michelangelo distributed the cast of his Sistine Chapel decoration pretty much along the line indicated here for art at large beginning, for his ancients, with God the Father (in five of the panels) and proceeding from Noah through the Prophets to Peter and Paul. In his *School of Athens* Raphael's older Greek philosophers spring directly from Michelangelo's models in the Sistine Chapel

Michaelangelo, *Ezekiel,* Musei Vaticani, Rome.

Michaelangelo, *Jeremiah,* Musei Vaticani, Rome.

as do his versions of God and characters from the Old Testament in the Biblical stories of the Vatican Loggia. But in spirit and beauty Correggio's apostles, evangelists, and fathers from the Cathedral at Parma really come next after Michelangelo.

Rubens's examples of all the foregoing, plus *Silenuses, Neptunes, River Gods, Adoring Kings, Jupiters,* and plain *Old Men,* are marvels in their own way, for the sheer painting of beards, on top of the customary miraculous execution we associate with the name of the greatest of all Lowlanders.

There is much less grandeur in the elderly thinkers Rembrandt so often elected to paint, but the images he created arouse a more intense interest on the viewer's part than do those of any other painter in history. All his subjects appear grave and far seeing. When in addition they bear the marks of the passage of time, the wisdom of the ages seems personified before us.

A final set of splendid old men, stemming directly from all these great precedents, but not in the least to be regarded as a pastiche, so autographic is every touch, was produced by Jean-Honoré Fragonard. These wonderful heads are the conventionalized old men of European art, but in their magnificent abruptness they testify to the force of that conception, because Fragonard turned them out (as he did everything) in no time whatsoever. They are prodigies of skill, but of artistic before naturalistic skill, yet with enough of the latter to avoid any risk of the dulness that stylization by itself always threatens.

Raphael, *Plato and Aristotle,* detail from *The School of Athens,*
Musei Vaticani, Rome.

Raphael, *Pythagoras* detail from *The School of Athens,* Musei Vaticani, Rome.

Raphael, *Heraclitus* detail from *The School of Athens,* Musei Vaticani, Rome

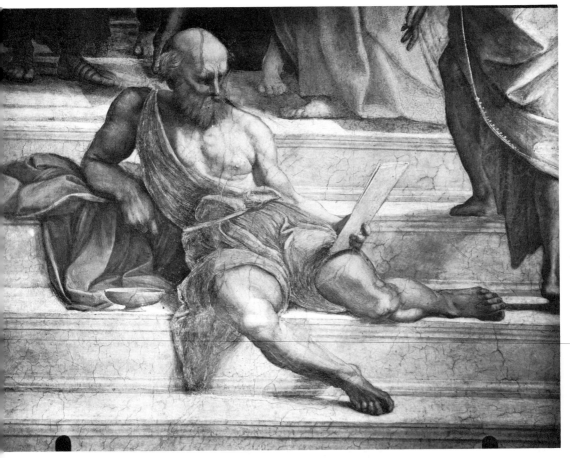

Raphael, *Diogenes* detail from *The School of Athens,* Musei
Vaticani, Rome.

Bernini, *Saints Ambrose and Athanasius* detail from *The Chair of Saint Peter,* Rome, Saskia/Editorial Photocolor Archives.

CHAPTER 6

The Virgin as Mother:
The Rustic Madonna

A mid-nineteenth-century painting shows Raphael, surrounded by his entourage, sketching a young girl and her baby by the roadside, evidently caught quite by accident in her fetching pose. We are given to understand that this represents the genesis of the idea of *The Madonna of the Chair*. What is really shown is the later painter's method of practice, not Raphael's. We have no reason to think Raphael ever made a sketch in his life of a sight or incident noted in passing that he thought might be put to artistic use. We know nothing of how he went about things, whether or not, in fact, he employed models at all. What it is safe to say is that his inspiration came from the pictures of others, improved on. A degree of that improvement was owed to a peculiarly keen appreciation of nature's beauty. Raphael did not substitute this beauty for his predecessors' conventions; rather, he enriched those conventions. His Madonnas were by all means truer to life than Perugino's and disposed themselves in more plausible landscapes, but they were not a whit less stylized and were as artificially arranged, if with more grace. In short, for what was new nothing old was sacrificed, and this combination of addition and retention was his magic formula.

69

That accounts for the success of Raphael's Madonnas as works of art. It was their unprecedented lifelikeness that captured the Renaissance public. Earlier Madonnas were doubtless loved for what they represented and, in any number of cases, for the appeal of the actual mother and child themselves. After Raphael, the earlier versions seemed extraordinarily unreal.

Raphael, *The Alba Madonna,* National Gallery of Art, Washington, Andrew W. Mellon Foundation.

Attitude, gesture, facial expression, high polish, all contributed to the degree of charm exerted. What gave these factors their special force was Raphael's turning away from the device of the Virgin as enthroned queen, though not before he had produced several beautiful examples in this vein. He was not the first to think of this, but he could recognize a great idea. The supreme formalist had no compunctions about seeking equal rank as a genre painter. His Virgin shown with a matchless technique as a rural mother conquered Europe.

The force of this is largely lost on us, because we have been nurtured on a century and a half of sentimental naturalism, unadulterated by any appreciable amount of style or order. What we see in Raphael's Madonnas is unrivaled finish, gorgeous pattern and irresistible grace. It is instructive to remember that this was not his whole intent.

Of Madonnas whose character of intimacy strikes a more responsive chord in the twentieth century, Leonardo da Vinci's come immediately to mind, with the *Madonna del Fiore* in the Hermitage in Leningrad a case in point. What sets the picture apart is the captivating head of the Virgin, still barely more than a child herself, looking infinitely less grave than the infant on her knee. The seraphic sweetness of her expression is owed the first genuine smile in the history of Western painting. Genuine, because it can be stated with no hesitation that all earlier apparent painted smiles are present through no fault of the artist. It is worth adding that when he completed this masterpiece the painter was not very far out of his own childhood.

If Leonardo was the pioneer in this dangerous area (for the smile on the painted countenance is always a hazard), the man who raised the smile to an ecstatic pitch that no subsequent painter has approached was Correggio. 71

Leonardo da Vinci, *Madonna dei Fiori*, State Hermitage Museum, Leningrad.

Correggio, *Madonna della Cesta,* The National Gallery, London.

Correggio, who defies explanation—a supreme master who remained in the provinces—made the smile, the most elusive of human expressions, the chief identifying feature of his work. Four hundred and fifty years after his death we are still enchanted by that smile. Yet these perfect smiles remain incidental to the hold his pictures have on us. If we limit our attention to his Madonnas—and it sometimes seems as if all his easel paintings are, in fact, Madonnas—it is safe to say that Correggio reached the outer limits of grace in movement. Nothing more beautiful can be imagined than the attitude and gesture of his *Madonna Adoring Her Baby,* in the Uffizi, nor could anything so beautiful be at the same time so lifelike as the *Mystic Marriage of Saint Catherine* in the Louvre.

In the greatest of all Christmas pictures, *La Notte* in Dresden shows the shepherds coming in the dark to the magically illuminated manger. While the painting itself, in its elaborateness, might almost be thought of as a Renaissance machine in the nineteenth-century sense of the word, the heart of the matter is another marvelous mother and baby, on top of all else, perfectly convincing in their rusticity.

CHAPTER 7

The Virgin Triumphant:
Madonna in Glory

The Virgin of the Counter Reformation inherited the naturalness, but not the humility or intimacy, of the Madonna as rural mother. The Virgin in the sky, after all, transcended humanity, and her representation required the accoutrements and bearing that indicated supremacy. This was the last word in the "paganism" that exercised Northern Europe to the point of the destruction of so much of its own art. Mary was not, however, Pallas Athene. She remained in touch with humanity by virtue of her origin. Still, in displaying her in her regal capacity the artists saw no reason to stint, and the miraculous element the subject permitted allowed for the pulling out of all stops. The Virgin was exalted in customary terms, but beyond any secular ruler.

Correggio set the pattern, with a vision of Paradise (in the dome of the Cathedral of Parma) made up of a so thickly enmeshed ring of saints and angels that it is difficult to single out the Virgin herself. Raphael's *Sistine Madonna* is composed with perfect arbitrariness. Curtains are drawn back to reveal the Virgin standing on the Globe before a background composed of the heads of baby angels,

Pierre-Paul Prud'Hon, *The Assumption of the Virgin,* The
Louvre, Paris. Photo Musées Nationaux.

Peter Paul Rubens, *The Assumption,* Courtesy The Princely
Collections of Liechtenstein.

while Saint Barbara and the Pope kneel before her on clouds. On a kind of sill at the base of the picture, the most famous pair of angels in the world gaze upwards adoringly, though their backs are actually to the Virgin. but the outward gazes of the angels was not the area of concern that would have troubled Raphael, with the picture held for generations to be the most beautiful ever painted.

In the way of similar judgments, when the Prussians were at the gates of Paris during the War of 1870, the work that was singled out of all the treasures in the Louvre as most important to protect from the enemy was Murillo's *Immaculate Conception*. This is not a reputation that has endured. On Assumptions alone, the world would probably agree that Titian's, in the Church of the Frari in Venice, is superior.

Tiepolo almost certainly painted more Madonnas in glory than anyone, simply by virtue of the quantity of ceilings he was responsible for. These ceilings were invariably well populated skies, more often than not the heavenly sky, presided over by the Virgin. All are magnificent and possessed of the rodomontade that adds to the charm, and detracts from the gravity, of Tiepolo.

In much of the same spirit, Tiepolo's younger Bavarian contemporary, the sculptor Ignaz Gunther, produced for the Parochial Church of Glatz an *Immaculate Conception* in polychrome, a gorgeous vision in blue and gold, and another in the Church of Saint Joseph in Starnberg. White against an explosion of golden rays, the Holy Child is supported on a golden globe by his mother, with Saint Joseph a step below. If these beautiful statues share much of the theatricality of Tiepolo it is fair to add that the actual pathos displayed in Gunther's faces moves us far more than Tiepolo's eye rolling and hand wringing.

Ignaz Gunther,
*Immaculate Concep-
tion,* Parochial
Church, Glatz.

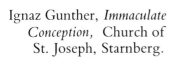

Ignaz Gunther, *Immaculate
Conception,* Church of
St. Joseph, Starnberg.

CHAPTER 8

The Sitter
As Hero

A large portion of the aristocracy of Europe keyed its assertion of primacy to a fancied link with the Roman imperial lineage, and the principal iconographical instrument of this was to lead off any display of ancestral portraits with that of Julius Caesar as the family founder, followed by his not so direct descendants and successors, the so-called Twelve Caesars of Suetonius.

Of these sets of bogus genealogies, those by Titian are the best known, but what is pertinent is that the individual items of this innocent exercise were regarded in the same light as the portraits of bonafide forbears. That is, position and character were what counted, not likeness. For one thing, it was a late development for the subject of a portrait to actually hold still for the artist. Presently, of course, identification would become of consequence, to match in importance the earlier concerns, rather than to supersede them. The chains of office, the coats of arms, the glimpses of domains, would survive well into the eighteenth century, as would regal bearing beyond that time.

Michelangelo, *Lorenzo de Medici,*
Medici Chapel, Church of
San Lorenzo, Florence.
Photo Lauros-Giraudon.

Michelangelo, *Giuliano de Medici,*
Medici Chapel, Church of
San Lorenzo, Florence.
Photo Lauros-Giraudon.

Giovanni Lorenzo Bernini, *Bust of Louis XIV*,
National Gallery of Art, Washington.
Samuel H. Kress Collection, 1943.

Hyacinthe Rigaud, *Louis XIV*, The Louvre, Paris.
Photo Musées Nationaux.

Human nature would see to it that very long ago, when naturalness became important to the painter himself, his patrons would begin to interest themselves in how he portrayed them. That source of intense aggravation to artists, the complaint about likeness, goes way back. The point at issue was that the sitter wanted there to be no uncertainty that he was, in fact, the splendid figure created by the artist. The first responsibility of the painter or sculptor remained celebration.

The supreme example of complete disregard of the obligation to produce a resemblance was Michelangelo's carving of Lorenzo and Giuliano de Medici as Ancient Romans, totally unrelated to anything known of their actual appearance. This august precedent would not be followed. In the next century what would be exclaimed over in Bernini's busts would be the sense conveyed of the living human presence of recognizable, extraordinarily recognizable, individuals. It must be added that there would be no diminishment here of the idea of personal force, which continued to be implied in the very theory of the portrait.

If Hyacinthe Rigaud may not have been the absolute keenest among his countrymen in the production of the likeness, only the greatest names can be brought forward as his rivals. Where his supremacy is uncontested is in the combining of his intensively studied faces with the full paraphernalia of nobility. Where all other portraitists leaned a little in one direction or the other, Rigaud exerted his tremendous powers equally. To the actual detriment of his reputation, this incomparable master of characterization turned out a body of portraits that are the richest in history in the material evidence of prestige. The effect is of an excess of the attributes of nobility. Rigaud's specialty was drapery, by which, we have to admit, he was carried away.

84

Maurice-Quentin de La Tour, *Madame de Pompadour,*
The Louvre, Paris. Photo Musées Nationaux.

One has to speculate as to whether his subjects could really have moved, or stood erect, under the weight of fabric he heaped on them. The idea of skimping hardly applies to an artist of such prodigality as Rigaud, but the very abundance of stuff crowded out the customary complement of architecture or landscape. The garments of Rigaud's figures were their settings as well.

Rigaud's masterpiece, and the foremost instance of the portrait as theatre and idol, was his *Louis XIV*. If this presentation of a short man as ten heads high is often made light of, the fact remains that it is a marvel of organization and rendering, with the ermine lining of the mantle cascading over the King's left arm a shape of rare beauty that would dominate the arrangement were it not for the central motif, the wonderful head and posture. This is a performance against which nothing of the same vein can be matched. We may, by all means, dislike it, but what we prefer has to be something entirely other.

The French portrait painters and sculptors of the century to follow could not improve on Rigaud's heads, but in lessening the emphasis on accessories they would make much more of their subjects as human beings. Again, the factor is balance, not realism, for what this generation, with Maurice-Quentin de La Tour and Jean-Antoine Houdon at the fore, offers us is a race, in aspect and expression, simply too gracious, intelligent, and attractive for the possibility of its existence to be seriously entertained.

Houdon, by virtue of his busts of Washington and Jefferson and Franklin so familiar to Americans as almost to qualify as a Founding Father himself, might be taken to be the very soul of objectivity, from the pains we know him to have gone to over exact resemblance. Nevertheless, we can measure the weaknesses unkind historians have

Maurice-Quentin de La Tour, *Manelli,* The Louvre, Paris. Photo Bulloz.

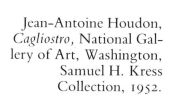

Jean-Antoine Houdon, *Cagliostro,* National Gallery of Art, Washington, Samuel H. Kress Collection, 1952.

Anthony Van Dyck, *Charles I,* The Louvre, Paris. Photo
Musées Nationaux.

brought to our notice as the chief part of Lafayette's makeup against Houdon's image of him as incomparable leader. Another marble vision, half sage and half saint, is of Cagliostro, in actuality all charlatan.

Houdon's great counterpart in two dimensions and color, La Tour, contributed his share of this intensely real, and partly fabulous, record of the ruling class of France on the eve of its destruction, in pastel, as often as not confining his effort to the head alone. That is, without a hint of the Order of the Golden Fleece or a view of a park with a vase, we know perfectly well the level of society that has been brought before us.

The old revolutionary, Jacques-Louis David, would depict a class new to the idea of having its picture painted. But however faithful in examining the features before him, and without the old emblems of authority, he would succeed in creating a record of sitters quite as clearly in charge of things as their overthrown predecessors.

Across the Channel, portraiture as we think of it stems entirely from the great Flemish immigrant, Anthony Van Dyck. With an innate talent and the example and instruction of Rubens, and with a taste formed by his study of Titian, Van Dyck created for all time the pattern of the aristocrat. Van Dyke was supreme over all the artists of the world, before or since, in conveying the idea of superiority by gesture and carriage. His armor, his skies, his architectural detail, above all his marvelous garments, could not be improved on, but Van Dyck's triumph was that they remained subordinate to his heads and hands. It is a mark of his power that two painters so unlike as Joshua Reynolds and Thomas Gainsborough, each a great master, should have been wholly formed out of his example. 89

Joshua Reynolds, *Banastre Tarleton,* The National Gallery,
London

Thomas Gainsborough, *The Morning Walk,* The National
Gallery, London.

Pierre-Paul Prud'hon, *Joséphine,* The Louvre, Paris. Photo
Musées Nationaux.

From the moment of its invention the camera had a great bearing on portrait painting. First, and most absolute, it made painting itself unnecessary as a means of preserving likenesses. Second, despite a stigma attached to the practice, the camera entered into the very process of portrait painting. Of equal weight, the photograph established in the lay mind an idea about appearance that nature unaided by the lens had never suggested, and that was inimical to any notion of pictorial style. If the original miracle of the invention was seen as the work of painting done by a machine, all too soon painting, and portrait painting in particular, was taken to be the making of photographs by hand.

With the actual standard a mechanical one, the concept of the portrait was reversed. Generalization and idealization were construed as falsification. Although portrait painting, by virtue of this, retained a sturdier link with actuality than any other branch of the art, the narrowing of its goal put it outside the central current of the culture of the West.

CHAPTER 9

The Anonymous Hero

The common man put in his appearance early in the history of oil painting. In northern Europe, where oil painting was invented, almost the first pictures so produced provide us glimpses of farmers in their fields, of life in the streets, of work under way. These are glimpses only. The tiny, if crystal clear, view we are offered of existence at the opening of the Renaissance is confined to backgrounds, distant at that. If the democratic impulse was strong, so was the sense of artistic propriety, and the central themes of Flemish art remained lofty ones, with the protagonists presented in aristocratic guise.

A century later, Pieter Brueghel brought the people to the fore. His ostensible subjects, *The Massacre of the Innocents, The Tower of Babel, The Fall of Icarus,* were the merest excuses for the assembling of a marvelous panorama of Flemish boisterousness. The convention, at Brueghel's hands, was turned inside out; the backgrounds of his pictures had to be searched through to locate his nominally principal characters.

Presently the peasant would become the main subject in a school of painting headed by Adriaen Brouwer and Adriaen van Ostade. The fact of this is remarkable enough in itself, but it should be noted that these little pictures cannot be thought of as realistic. The figures depicted in them are given an unmistakable comic emphasis. No dignity of bearing is allowed them, nor are they shown engaged in serious, or for that matter any, tasks. Their habitat is the tavern; they smoke and drink and play a little music. The intended effect was of dissoluteness, with the paintings themselves called, in case there is any doubt in the matter, pictures of boors.

It was Jean-François Millet, in the middle of the nineteenth century, who first accorded the laborer full artistic attention. The heir of Correggio and Prud'hon, Millet saw life a good deal less cheerfully than they, but in their terms of form. If his figures were heroic, he employed very old devices to make them so. In the company of the masters his pictures strike almost nothing of an innovating note. The gravity of his field workers' bearing and movement, their large and generalized contours, are identifying characteristics Millet shared with few contemporaries. He was very much an observer of life around him, but what he saw he put to the service of his art, not the reverse.

Perhaps because he remained in the city, we are even more conscious of tradition in Daumier's pictures than in Millet's. While in surface and touch Daumier's canvases were dissatisfying to a public that set store by finish, his passengers on the early railroads, his laundresses and itinerant clowns, were seen within the tenets of conventionalized pictorial prescription. This was modified by the painter's manifest sympathy for his subjects, but little was owed to observation. His heart, not his eye, was engaged by the spectacle of the underside of Parisian life.

If sentiment, based on slight evidence, makes Daumier a man of the people, that seems fair enough, but there

Jean-François Millet, *The Gleaners,* The Louvre, Paris. Photo Lauros-Giraudon.

Jean-François Millet, *The Sower,* Museum of Fine Arts,
Boston, Gift of Q. A. Shaw. © 1979 Museum of Fine Arts.

Honoré Daumier, *The Laundress,* The Louvre, Paris,
Photo Bulloz.

is not a line from his hand in existence that has the look of having been drawn out of doors. The standard interpretation of his power is that he possessed a prodigious memory. Insofar as this is so, that memory was of paintings, not of what today we call visual experience. Daumier was a cartoonist nursed on painting; his strength in either field came from his mastery of the deepest principles of the other. His daily lithograph for the newspaper was composed in the rhythmic forms of Tintoretto or Rubens, and he roughed out the figures for his paintings with the unaffected ease developed in a career given over to the illustration of jokes.

The third famous man of the age to apply old-fashioned methods to hitherto neglected subjects was Gustave Courbet. Where he parted company with Millet and Daumier was that he devoted his considerable gifts and a technique handed down through the centuries to extraordinarily mundane purpose. In limiting himself entirely to the most prosaic transcription of what he laid eyes on he was the first painter of any stature to deliberately jettison the concept of painting as an instrument of enhancement.

It is sometimes suggested that we had a kind of domestic Courbet of our own in the United States, Winslow Homer. The thought is that, in the midst of Victorian prettification and sentimentality, here was a man who confined himself to the unvarnished recording of what was before him. Some of the rare quotations from the taciturn New Englander might appear to support such a view. The test is his work. His pictures are the most keenly designed, and hence arbitrarily arranged, of any American's, so the notion of purely factual reporting on his part is without any substance to begin with. More, his popularity as an illustrator with the public of the Gilded Age makes clear

Winslow Homer, *The Berry Pickers*, Colby College Museum of Art.

Winslow Homer, *The Gale*, Worcester Art Museum, Worcester, Mass.

Winslow Homer, *The Fog Warning,* Museum of Fine Arts, Boston. Otis Norcross Fund.

Winslow Homer, *The Life Line,* Philadelphia Museum of Art, George W. Elkins Collection.

Winslow Homer, *The Herring Net,* Art Institute of Chicago.
Photo, Courtesy, Art Institute of Chicago.

that there was something present in his work besides objectivity. His specialty was rural America, and the vision he conveyed to the readers of *Harper's Weekly* was of effortless farming, with what little work needed to be done, sheep tending or berry picking, managed by children, and in a picnic atmosphere. The pictures he painted were of the same flavor until, stimulated by new sights, he produced his water colors of the English coast. No longer bucolic, they were not a jot more realistic. What he served up was the drama of the peril of the sea, personified by the splendid girls who waited out the storm on shore. His approach was that of the purest monumentality. Not least, his people all looked alike, and the effect was conveyed by the gravity of their carriage and largeness of contour.

More overtly dramatic pictures followed. *Fog Warning, The Life Line, The Herring Net,* are stories of imminent danger. The viewer's concern is heightened by Homer's reserve; his characters do not wave their arms, or grimace, or point, as in more commonplace pictures, or perhaps even in real life. In that sense his men of the sea are ennobled by their stoicism, a somewhat more literary consideration than that of the girls on the Tynemouth cliffs.

Homer's hunters and woodsmen of the Adirondacks are a far cry from the Indian guide unable to make a fourth at bridge. The heroic nature of these denizens of the forest is implied by the magnificence of the setting they are shown as intimately part of. That magnificence itself is increased by the presence of these obviously brave, wise, generous types. Again, as with the earlier farmers, it is not at all apparent that much actual work is under way.

Homer, then, was hardly a celebrator of labor, honest or oppressed. It would probably be true to say that he had a kind of ideal, abstract, personality in his mind that, in

Winslow Homer, *The Osprey's Nest,* Sterling and Francine
Clark Art Institute, Williamstown, Mass.

Winslow Homer, *Old Friends,* Worcester Art Museum,
Worcester, Mass.

light of his pronounced intolerance for most live human beings, was best typified by strangers seen outdoors, at a distance. But the stature of Homer, or any artist, is not owed to sociological factors. What is of consequence is that his conception of nature held truer to the central thread of Western art than that of any other American save Thomas Sully. His little figures in contemporary garb breathe far more Hellenic air than all the toga-clad Columbias and Spirits of Transportation or Electricity that, from the 1890s on, were to flow from the brushes and chisels of a later generation. What is to be regretted is that it occurred to no one to make use of the one genuinely monumental pictorial outlook in the country in any great civic project. Homer's command of space and movement would have made him the foremost decorator of his age.

There were of course instances of people shown doing a little work prior to the nineteenth century. Caravaggio, alone, introduced something of a class issue by underlining the plebeian origin of the casts of his religious dramas. If the question were simply one of models, Rembrandt would be the great exemplar. And perhaps he should be. He was supreme, after all, in imparting distinction to his sitters unaided by accoutrements or setting.

In the immediate context, however, the great master who is to the purpose is Vermeer. His contribution was to exalt not work (in the social sense) but mundane gesture. Letters are read and milk poured in interiors of perfect beauty, without a touch of grandiloquence or affectation. Vermeer's triumph lies in the establishment of an ideal balance; that is, that the action performed is precisely worthy of the marvelous form given the recording of it. What we really expect to be shown us by painters is the magnanimity of kings, and we cannot help but feel a faint sense   107

Jan Vermeer, *The Astronomer,* Photo Lauros–Giraudon,
Rothschild Collection.

Jan Vermeer, *The Lacemakers,* The Louvre, Paris. Photo
Musées Nationaux.

of dissatisfaction when more prosaic subjects seem not to warrant the trouble gone to over them. With Vermeer, no such contradiction ever asserts itself.

There are plenty of works ostensibly showing what we might describe as thought being taken. Of all these starers and brow furrowers none comes to mind that is completely free of a comic touch, with the most famous statue of modern times, actually labelled *The Thinker,* the ideal example of this. But Vermeer's *Geographer* and *Astronomer,* with no such lofty intention so much as hinted at, convey the very air of reflection by a magic combination of physical atmosphere and gesture.

What we have in these pictures of subjects who are not themselves movers and shakers is, by virtue of that, what might be defined as a purely imaginative art. The old ruling class, whatever the possible shortcomings in appearance of its individual members, was the genuine article to begin with, and simply expected its painters to make this evident.

CHAPTER 10

The Comedians

Holman Hunt said of Sir Joshua Reynolds that he was to Jacques-Louis David as Pegasus to a Percheron. Most of us would agree with this unkind comparison. But Sir Joshua Reynolds himself described David's *Death of Socrates* as the greatest picture ever painted. Perhaps he was simply carried away for the moment. Still, something of the central current of Western art does flicker in the history pictures of 1800. In addition to the lofty purpose behind these always didactic works they are the products of an intensity by which we cannot help but be stirred. On another plane their very scale is intimidating. As a class (mural painting apart), the history pictures are the most ambitious ever undertaken.

Yet in regarding these splendid creations chiefly as wonders we are slightly outside the realm of esthetics. There is, in fact, an emphasis here different from the familiar one. The figures are no longer emblematic but are particular individuals. The powerful drawing displayed had as its goal exact transcription. Grace and movement have been left behind. It is true that David and his pupils imparted a marked degree of statuesqueness to the protagonists of their

Jacques-Louis David, *The Death of Socrates,* The Metropolitan
Museum of Art, Wolfe Fund, 1931.

Jacques-Louis David, *The Oath of the Horatii,*
The Louvre, Paris. Photo Bulloz.

heroic dramas, but it is the stoniness and immobility of sculpture that is conveyed, not its warmth and grandeur.

These remarkable paintings, which can in all fairness be characterized as essentially inartistic, signalled the termination of what has been identified here as the main concern of European culture, the celebration of Man. In its place was substituted not even the honoring of the individual but his mere depiction. The still idealistic tone of the French Revolution and the Napoleonic Empire would soon be dropped. What survived was the particularlized rendering of nature. In the ensuing century the theme of art would be the differences between people and objects, rather than the common factors. The generalized view of nature was no more.

To come down to cases, a characteristic nineteenth century painting represented specific persons at specific moments and places, a goal shared alike by impressionist and academician whose disputes were over method, not purpose. The ideal head had been succeeded by the exact likeness. It need hardly be added that, for practical purposes, these considerations hold true to this day, insofar as actuality is taken to be the subject of painting.

The question of purpose is outside that of quality. Countless pictures executed in the last hundred and fifty years were superior to any number of earlier ones in skill and appeal. But however interesting and admirable the results might be, the prosaic tone dictated by a narrowed outlook made impossible the lyricism that had been an inherent and conscious ingredient of occidental art since its inception. The main thread had been lost.

Drawing was brought to a very high level of precision. There was a vast increase of inventiveness in the choosing of subjects. The limiting, so to put it, of the artist's vision gave his work an apparent keenness lacking in the products of the generalized view of his predecessors. The universal test of art became, before all else, fidelity to immediate fact. Nature was no longer the great instrument at the disposal of the painter or sculptor for the fulfillment of his ends; its duplication was itself the end. Stylization and arrangement, throughout history the chief staples of practice, were now condemned on the moral ground of falsity.

The age was notoriously sentimental, and in nothing more than its art, but the cultivation of sentiment was the individual artist's problem. What he was drilled in was exactness. The pathetic work might be best loved, but the mirror of nature was the most esteemed. Nor were the academicians alone in this. The impressionists' contention was that theirs was an even more precise, and hence more narrowly focussed, truth.

Sir John Millais is the perfect example. The stories in his pictures still touch us after a hundred years, but in his time he was revered as an old master on the strength of his intense naturalism. The requirement, imposed by school and gallery, and even governments, was reinforced by popular preference.

The escape was the ancient one, the display by the artist of other than serious intent. The cartoonist, in particular, was expected to skirt actuality on principle. In England John Tenniel, the great illustrator of *Alice in Wonderland,* entertained the readers of *Punch* for sixty years with political wood engravings peopled with figures conceived in the purest terms of the European pictorial prescription, not least in dealing very largely in allegory. Tenniel's strict adherence to the picture plane, his generous contours, the stateliness of his figures' movement, and the harmonious

"COUNTING HER CHICKS!"

SCENE—*Besika Bay.*

BRITANNIA (*to the Old Hen*). "DON'T FLUTTER YOURSELF!—*THEY'LL* TAKE CARE OF THEMSELVES!"

John Tenniel, *Counting Her Chicks,* Cartoon from *Punch.*
Author's Collection.

THE FRENCH ANDROMEDA;

OR, WANTED, A PERSEUS.

John Tenniel, *The French Andromeda,* Cartoon from *Punch.*
Author's Collection.

assembling of those figures, combined to make his little weekly drawing the most artistic product of the Kingdom, with his Raphaelesque composition beyond the powers of his famous British contemporaries. It is only fair to add that these famous painters were Tenniel's admirers to a man and that Ruskin himself held him akin to Tintoretto.

Across the Channel another great man, quite content to be the Parisians' favorite cartoonist, was making use of convention to the complete exclusion of observation. Honoré Daumier demonstrated more breadth in drawing than had been seen since Fragonard. That drawing, too, was employed in powerful figure arrangements no other Frenchman could approach, and the artist himself was accorded what might be called affectionate indulgence on the assumption that he was parodying old-fashioned style.

More extravagantly praised by his contemporaries than Daumier, while at the same time held up to scorn precisely because he made so bold as to challenge the painters in their own field, Gustave Doré possessed a superhuman command of the pencil. Imbued almost from babyhood with the ingredients of Western style, everything he undertook, from a tiny tail-piece for a page to a canvas thirty feet high, was larger, and more volcanic in movement, than life itself. Doré's internationally celebrated illustrations of the classics were shot through with humor, making them acceptable to the most cultivated taste. It was the note of seriousness in his painting that set critical opinion against him. Grandeur and breadth had become, for Frenchmen, laughing matter. As for Daumier's much more modestly scaled paintings, they were barely noticed in his lifetime. In the light of the most fundamental definition of what constitutes the art of the West, nineteenth-century painting fails to qualify. But Tenniel, Daumier,

Gustave Doré, *Puss-in-Boots,* wood engraving. Illustration
from *The Fables of La Fontaine*. Author's Collection.

Gustave Doré, wood engraving *"Satan's Remorse"* from
Milton's *Paradise Lost*. Author's Collection.

Honoré Daumier, lithograph for *Charivari*.

Honoré Daumier, *The Republic,* The Louvre, Paris. Photo
Musées Nationaux

and Doré filled the specifications. Nor was this mere literal compliance with convention. Their individual powers were such that only the most brilliant names of the previous centuries are to be compared with theirs.

There is a postscript to the foregoing. In our own time another *Punch* illustrator and cartoonist, Ernest Shepard, drew and composed with a fluency and grace no twentieth-century painter could rival. Shepard was a master, too, of that great pictorial device, the human figure in defiance of gravity. Shepard, perhaps from the very nature of his calling (like Tenniel, making liberal use of allegory), presented his soaring maidens with perfect plausibility and grace.

The last great master of motion as such flourished, fittingly enough, in France, in the decades that spanned the turn of the century. Jules Chéret may very well be only the second best poster designer in the world after Toulouse-Lautrec, and his work may be charged with grave shortcomings on other accounts, but even among the greatest artists his superior in depicting motion is not to be found. The tribute Forain paid Tiepolo on his return from Italy was that the great Venetian's frescoes had reminded him of Chéret.

Ernest Shepard, *Freedom's Task,* Political Cartoon from *Punch.*
Author's Collection.

Jules Chéret, *Loïe Fuller,* poster.

CHAPTER 11

―――

Some Further Considerations

The historical circumstance is that well into the nineteenth century there was hardly such a thing as a painting or statue to which the foregoing stipulations failed to apply. In that light, narrowness or exclusiveness has nothing to do with the matter. Illustrated by great examples, universal practice has been described. If a limited number worked at the highest level, that was entirely due to restricted opportunity. The profession has always been a difficult one, but the artist who had a hard time did not suffer in the Bohemian sense; he was not discriminated against because he had elected to go against prevailing understanding of what art was taken to be. It simply crossed no one's mind that any such option existed. Talent by all means asserted itself in individual ways, but toward a commonly agreed to goal.

On the eve of our own times, say a century and a half ago, this ceased to be. Depending on how we look at it, a degree of freedom was given to the artist that he had never before enjoyed, or it could be said that a burden was laid on him that has been an immense hindrance ever since to creative activity itself. The choice was not offered him, but the obligation was incurred by him, to decide, assisted only by contentious parties, what his very calling was understood to be. The inhibiting nature of this was that the choice to be made, however radical or conservative, was bound to be a minority one, with a lifelong defensive effort required by and attached to the making of it. It could be said that the inherent uncertainties of the philosopher's task were added to (and an interference with) the artist's creative task.

A moral or intellectual advance may be seen in this, but both these criteria are outside the imaginative, emotional, creative realm. An artist, by the very nature of his calling, is constantly making decisions, but it is a dissipation of this faculty to employ it outside the area of actual practice.

When the visiting exhibition of works of art from Dresden moved on to other cities from the National Gallery in Washington, one picture, because of the difficulty of transporting it, remained behind. *Quos Ergo* or *Neptune Taming the Waters,* by Rubens, was shoe-horned into the room housing the Rubens paintings belonging to the Gallery itself.

We are so geared to books that we tend to disregard size in artistic matters. Veronese's *Apotheosis of Venice* and Vermeer's *Milkmaid,* set alongside one another are compared by the differences in movement and stylization, and color and form, that manifest themselves in matching reproductions. But the real distinction between the two is that the *Marriage Feast* is huge and the *Milkmaid* pocket-size. That is, in taking art entirely into the area of study and classification, we have let actuality go by the board. Physical presence and conspicuousness, which might very well be thought of as the principal esthetic considerations because they are absolute in determining effectiveness, have

Paolo Veronese, *The Apotheosis of Venice,*
The Ducal Palace, Venice. Photo EPA.

simply been lost sight of. *Quos Ergo* was a nice corrective of this. The largest picture ever brought into the National Gallery, or for that matter Washington itself, put down in the midst of a set of relatively small (as those things go) works by Rubens, it was nothing less than overpowering. And the fact that all other pictures within view were identical in outlook and execution confined comparison to scale. *Quos Ergo* was set apart in no way except that it was enormous.

There was even more to this. Gigantic in itself, it was a single item in a series. So the accomplishment to be measured was the spectacle before the viewer's eyes multiplied several times.

It goes without saying that the ordinary questions of authorship hardly apply here. Only a crowd could operate on the scale required. Design itself becomes secondary. But the fact of many hands working together to turn out not merely *Quos Ergo,* but its like in quantity is less an explanation of a phenomenon than a wonder in itself. How could such an army have been assembled?

It is customary to speak (sometimes with a note of disdain) of Rubens presiding over a sort of factory. But what a factory! And what a product! For pictorial schemes, however devised, to be brought to realization in this pitch of finish and splendor is as astonishing as the apparent ease with which Rubens conceived those schemes to begin with.

Our own age has a prejudice in favor of autographic works, that is, those brimming with evidence of the individual creator's touch. Fair enough, but there are only so many masters, and the great ages are to be identified as much by the abundance of great works turned out as by the beauty of those works, an abundance created by some kind of system not exactly of mass production, but of production expanded beyond any single designer's powers.

Uncertainty as to what displays the actual touch of Rubens is a matter of academic concern. What the rest of us can be grateful for is that the works of Rubens, one of the pleasures of life, are in every museum. To more artistic purpose, in their own time they filled up the cities of Antwerp and Brussels and a good portion of the Flemish countryside. If anything is to be regretted, it is that they are not still in their original settings, making up a pictorial harmony the like of which exists in no other country, before or since.

The off-hand assumption would have to be that Rubens himself was a great organizer and teacher. But we might wonder whether time and energy given over to management would have been compatible with the quantity of undoubtedly autographic works Rubens has left us. The question is an idle one. It was unity of outlook and acceptance of a general prescription of style and form that accounted for the fact of Flemish talent working along a single line, and hence perfectly susceptible of being employed in concert on projects beyond the scope of individuals. And only with this unanimity would anything resembling what was the case here have been possible.

The least emphasis on personal expressiveness, or novelties of method, or stylistic innovation, would have undone the whole operation. That these represent the prevailing artistic ideas of the past two hundred years simply points up the moral of our story.

It is not that these ideas are fallacious in themselves; any concern is legitimate. The weakening and divisive factor is their substitution for the deeper currents of thought and inspiration that bind an art to the society that produces it. 131

There is, however, a further consideration in regard to *Quos Ergo*. The extraordinary fact about this giant picture (and its settings, of which it was but a part) is that it was turned out as a piece of street decoration, a temporary outdoor wall hanging to grace the reception in Antwerp of the Archduke Ferdinand of Austria, the newly appointed governor. That is, heroic and monumental as it is to our eyes, it was a short notice production not intended to survive its use. That it is still in existence is due to the Archduke's delight in the honor tendered him. He declined a money donation by the city in favor of the gift of the canvases that had lined the route of his approach to the city.

From the circumstance it follows that the whole enterprise could have represented nothing less than the most intense and sustained effort, with limited time and tremendous dimensions dictating this. By the same token, anything in the way of reflection and study would have been out of the question. And an off-the-cuff performance, which this would accordingly have been, could only have been the product of what was second nature to the participants. In short, for all the physical labor the immense task obviously entailed, the artistic part was accomplished with no strain at all. That is, whatever might have gone wrong with the mechanical side of the project, the pictures themselves were a success from the start. And nothing did go wrong, because attention could be entirely concentrated on execution.

Rubens' powers as a composer might appear the chief factor here, along with the authority of his personal style. But that style was no more than a distillation of the style of the West itself and his design a command of devices of pictorial arrangement familiar to everybody. Nothing he laid out for his collaborators would have been in the way of novelty. His stature as a master was simply owed to his fluency within indicated bounds.

He prescribed his schemes in oil sketches that were very liberally interpreted in their enlargement. The likelihood is strong that in some cases he limited himself to a few words of description of what he expected. The great chef d'atelier might almost be thought of as a kind of editor, who suggested what he had in mind and then corrected what was submitted to him. Rubens' unrivaled brilliance as a draftsman and colorist accounted for the peculiar distinction of the finished result, but the phenomenon we are examining, supremely beautiful pictures, overwhelming in magnitude, painted at a spectacular pace, requires a more fundamental explanation.

The secret was no more (or less) than the force of style, and the subscribing by all parties to the central idea, the glorification of the human body. That is, everyone in the studio who handled chalk or brush worked toward this end, as everyone in Antwerp, or for that matter Europe, expected them to. Animated by a sort of emergency—in this case the Viceroy's arrival in town—they simply geared their customary routines to a higher pitch. But that customary routine was the idealization and generalization of what was depicted. In so doing, they were led by the presiding genius, but they took their task to be the emulation of the Greeks and Romans and Italians, with Rubens no more than a guide.

In William R. Ware's syllabus (published in 1893) of his course at Columbia University, we are provided with a method of instruction in architecture of a century ago. At first glance the program might appear severe. In fact, nothing could be easier. The beginner, with plates, not objects, placed before him, is not required to try to repro-   133

Peter Paul Rubens, *The Deposition,* Antwerp Cathedral.

duce them free-hand, or even with ruler and compass, mechanically. All that is asked of him, in connection with the models offered, is to trace them. Presently, of course, he will go beyond this, but it is noteworthy that this very low level of imitativeness was the first step in learning to draw at a time when skill in drawing, on a wide scale, had been developed to the highest degree ever reached.

When the great private collections, through bountifulness on their owners' part, or confiscation by revolution, were nominally opened to the public, the public benefit was taken to be the education of the artist. That is, the masterpieces, hitherto inaccessible to the student, were now made available to anyone interested in copying them. The layman (so long as by his conduct or numbers he did not disturb the painters) might be allowed to have a look around, but his accommodation was by no means the main idea.

Hubert Robert's series of pictures of the interior of the Louvre at the time of the Revolution, both as it was and as he thought it ought to be, illustrates this. The long halls resemble crowded harbors in sailing times, with the copyists' canvases taking up every foot of space, and hardly a visitor in sight. Seventy years later, in Winslow Homer's engraving for *Harper's Weekly,* we are shown the same spectacle: an army of painters with, in the distance, a pair of gendarmes as the only other humans. Presumably their presence was to maintain this exclusiveness. Today, it might be noted, the shoe is on the other foot; the museum guard's responsibility is to see that the very occasional copyist (never more than one to a gallery) in no way discommodes the visitors. But the French government went beyond protection; it supported the copyists by the purchase of their efforts. If the ostensible purpose here was the distribution of the acquired works to provincial institutions, the real intent was to see that copying was kept up, as the very life-blood of the supremacy of French art.

This was not the government's only step toward that end. The successful contestant for the Prix de Rome (which was won by an original work) was required to turn in, as the crowning product of his three years of application at the Villa Medici, a copy of an assigned Italian masterpiece.

What this testifies to is that with the breakdown of the atelier system, copying became the universally acknowledged device for learning the secrets, such as they are, of the practice of painting and sculpture, and for the carrying forward of that practice.

For the student, copying was coupled with conventional instruction in school, and, presently, the latter would entirely supplant the former. It is of the merest speculative interest why this came to be. What is of consequence is that the decline of copying coincided exactly with the collapse of a consistently sustained outlook in European art. There came into being a kind of collective uncertainty as to the very nature of painting and sculpture.

Oral communication can serve to convey ideas of execution and conception. Repetition by the student can lead to the command of them, but acceptance, perhaps all to the good, remains optional. The artist is very loosely bound by his teacher's guidance and example. But there is more to art than thought and choice. And copying instills in us an instinctive and deep link to the matter duplicated wholly outside conscious decision on the copyist's part.

It might appear that what is being weighed here is the merit or usefulness of a kind of archaic chore. Would it even be imaginable, after all, that the youthful artist, long freed from it, would submit to this ancient discipline? Any such formulation has the whole matter backward. The peculiar fact is that the universal early manifestation of talent is copying. Where direction is called for is to wean the child away from what is taken to be too exclusive a preoccupation with this single artistic activity. That is, copying is instinctive, and the gifted simply display this by being better at it than their young contemporaries. If they keep it up after their companions lose interest, it is partly because of the greater enjoyment more successful efforts offer, largely because of the attention these efforts win.

To make of copying a moral issue is absurd, though it has by all means been done. Twentieth-century dogma explicitly condemns it. What is worth remarking on is that copying shares with other sin the stigma of being the product of natural impulse. It is this which makes it so hard for the virtuous to completely stamp it out. Originality certainly ought to be encouraged, in fact has to be encouraged, because it is not in the least instinctive, is rare and wonderful when it shows up, and accordingly perfectly unnatural.

Apart from the question of its evil or beneficial effects, the dominating circumstance is that copying is a great pleasure. This bears on its prevention or promotion. However frowned on by the authorities, with actual obstacles put in his way by the museums themselves (long divorced from their ancient role in the matter), the furtive copyist is still to be found at his easel. If opinion were reversed, with copying approved of, the least of difficulties would arise in setting students to the task. The problem might very well be to get them to do anything else.

The historic method of the transmission of style from one generation to another was the duplication of the master's work by his apprentices and assistants. It might appear that this was too inglorious a process to be called art instruction. This is true enough. The goal was not the development of anyone's talent; on the proprietor's mind was the widest possible circulation of his own works. Within this system, strong personalities, or particular gifts, might make themselves apparent, but anything along this line was remote from the purpose.

For the members of what today we would call a staff, the furthest thing from anyone's mind was the idea of the various individual contributions to a finished result being recognizable. The central task each party addressed himself to was the simulation of another's touch. This might seem the very formula for the suppression of individuality, and perhaps it was, but every great master was the product of exactly this discipline.

Part and parcel of any tradition is the means for carrying it on, or there is no tradition. What has been described here, the mimicry by the novice of the veteran, has served that office for the art of the entire world until very recent times, and the elementary demonstration of its indispensability is that when its practice ceases, tradition and style cease. So regarded, to weigh the suitability of slavish imitation (as it is construed to be) is beside the point. The issue is personal preference, and the obvious answer for the would-be artist jealous of his freedom, is to choose another calling, though he might not find, at that, very many other callings that welcome beginners' innovations. They have their own traditions and styles.

It might appear too prosaic, or even frivolous, to speak of the only proper preparation for a lifetime of creative activity as on-the-job training, but that is, in fact, what it amounts to. Participation by the artist, from the very start of his career, in the putting together of complete works   139 of art, as opposed to the studies of fragments of nature that are the staples of the art school, is infinitely more to the individual's advantage in developing breadth of vision, the widest possible range of skills, and a command of the mundane aspects of artistic production. But the end sought, in light of society's needs, is not the youthful aspirant's benefit. However much we are disciplined to think it so, the worthy national or cultural goal is not a host of famous artists. Beauty alone is of serious social purpose. All else is in the realm of hobby, or dilettantism, or display, and outside the serious concern of the public, nor in any way to its benefit. The real usefulness of the atelier system is that it maintains the continuity of aesthetic principles, and wonderfully multiplies the actual number of works of art. However much it might conform to our notions of democracy, it is far less to the general benefit for a dozen artists each to work toward his own goals than for eleven of them to fulfill those of the twelfth.

The scale of Tiepolo's output was the result of the participation of his sons and an accomplished associate, the architectural specialist Mengozzi-Colonna. Would we be better off if each of these had pursued an independant career? Long after Veronese's death, his studio carried on its customary practice. Is this to be regretted?

Apprenticeship, that is, working in exchange for instruction, is not only out of keeping with the uses of our times; it is against the law. That might suffice to put any notion of its revival beyond discussion. But it is so much the essential element in sustaining across any appreciable measure of time a consistent body of artistic ideas that it has to be considered, whatever the obstacles to its realization. The apparent alternative is the school, but the school is the chief instrument of the enfeeblement of tradition.

Giovanni Battista Tiepolo, *The Deposition,* The National
Gallery, London.

The usefulness of the aid given Tiepolo (more to ourselves than even Tiepolo in accounting for the volume of his work in existence) ought to be self-evident. But it is to the purpose to note that, in his turn, Tiepolo too was an apprentice, and to several painters, at that. One of these was Sebastiano Ricci, in his own right a famous man in his time. Tiepolo came to excel his master in every respect. He drew infinitely better, to begin with; he imbued his figures with wonderful grace, where Ricci was simply clumsy. In fact, at this distance removed, no serious comparison can be maintained between the two. But what is significant is that, over a very long career Tiepolo, who by his very incandescence blinds us to the existence of immediate predecessors and followers, never put down a line, or entertained a pictorial thought, that would have struck his old maestro as in any way novel. His schemes differed in no fundamental way from Ricci's, the conventions of his drawing were identical. Quality apart, it would be very difficult to describe Tiepolo's and Ricci's bodies of work in a way that would distinguish one from the other.

That is, the measure of Tiepolo's matchless supremacy was confined entirely to sheer excellence, a fluency of command of standing conventions of form and style, and of pencil and brush, such as had not been seen for a century. The individuality that accompanied this was the merest matter of what might be called calligraphic touch, identifiable habits of practice that no more than added to the charm of Tiepolo's fundamental mastery, without being in the least the substance of that mastery.

CHAPTER 12

Epilogue

The effort in these pages has been to establish the essential character of Occidental painting and sculpture. One usefulness in this might be to induce a little modesty in regard to the difference most of us instinctively see, or at least feel, between the limited, simple nature of alien cultures (however beautiful the product of these cultures) and the rich complexity of our own. But that was not the intent. We are free to regard ours as superior to all other art on the planet. The premise here is that if that superiority exists, it owes nothing to variousness. Moreover, that variousness works against actual artistic fulfillment.

Our initial argument was that, in turning our attention to the work of societies other than our own, we find it almost impossible to identify individuals, nations, even eras. We will go a little further and suggest that it is not simply unfamiliarity operating in this. Those distinctions are of no real consequence to those perfectly aware of them. And the homogeneity by which we are so captivated is directly due this disregard of factors which, among ourselves, we lay chief emphasis on.

In the West, personality, national characteristics, history, are all brought to the fore in judgment. Each is interesting; none is of the least artistic weight. But if it might appear harmless enough for critics, curators, professors, historians, dealers, to steer clear of fundamental esthetic considerations, this is not quite the case. The lecturing, criticism, instruction, salesmanship, chronicling, categorizing, that almost submerge, by their volume, artistic activity itself, are not lost upon the air. They set the intellectual tone. There is a vast educational structure, an almost frenzied encouragement of appreciation, constantly percolating criticism, classification, explanation, with an increasing physical plant for the accommodation of all this peripheral movement, remote from actual creation.

If there is a complaint it is not on the score of the amount of wealth and energy directed toward art, but on the tiny quantity of actual works that result from all this, and of these works, the minuteness of the portion that provides any general satisfaction. The remedy would be, first, for the generous public and private support that now goes to the academic, literary, and curatorial side of art to be diverted to the patronage of painting and sculpture themselves. But if this simply accounted for a vast increase in the number of random works of art, innovative and traditional, skilfull and inept, acceptable and offensive, entertaining and boring, the gamuts that are now spanned, the artists at large would be in a much more comfortable state, but our artistic stature would be raised by not an iota.

The only prospect, in the twentieth century (as in every other) would be for that sponsorship, and the creative activity itself, to be directed toward a common end. Whatever that end, the fact of a general effort transcending

144

that of the individual, of competitiveness along a single line, of a wide concern for the realization of that end, would lend immense strength to the esthetic force of the age.

If our whole manner of thinking is against any such unanimity, the fact remains that there has been no era of the least artistic consequence in the history of the world that failed to meet these conditions. Whatever great age we conjure up immediately illustrates the circumstances described. Only idle vanity would suggest that this fails to apply to ourselves.

On the premise, then, that ours can hardly be free from the requirements met by every other civilization, the purpose of outlining here what is taken to be the special nature of Western painting and sculpture is to mark a path along which the artist must proceed. That path may very well be challenged but, in that case, another must be laid down.